Appalachian Recipes
Clay County, Kentucky

by

Linda Roberts Sibley

Introduction

My family roots run deep in Clay County, Kentucky as Dillion Asher is my 4th great-grandfather. Dillion was the keeper of Kentucky's first toll gate at Pineville. Around 1799 he built a log cabin on the site now known as the Red Bird Mission in Beverly. Also, I am from the families of Roberts, Sizemore, Davidson, Hacker, Gay, Napier, Begley, and others that settled Clay County, Kentucky in the early 1800's.

I was born 1948 in Manchester, Clay County, Kentucky. I guess you would say we were poor, but I didn't realize it. We always had plenty of food on the table. I can remember my grandmother Avis Napier Roberts preparing breakfast of fried fat-back bacon, eggs, biscuits, and a huge bowl of gravy. Grandmother was not a fancy cook, but she could put food on the table for her eleven children.

Mother Malvery Roberts Begley is a wonderful cook. Still my favorite meal I remember her preparing is soup beans, fried potatoes with onion, and cornbread.

The first memory I have cooking is at about 12 years of age making Mother's Cookies. I made these cookies for Christmas this year – almost 60 years later.

I married a Texan in 1968 and moved to Texas. It took me a long time to appreciate Texas. In the first years of our marriage I would cry because I missed the mountains. Mac would take me to Mountain Peak, which is one of the highest points in Ellis County, and say he was sorry but this is the only mountain nearby. I would cry and tell him it was not even a hill.

In 1974 I began working for the City of Midlothian. First in the police department and later as court administrator. I worked there for 28 years. Later I decided to run for political office as Justice of the Peace and was the first, and still only, woman ever elected in Precinct #4.

I would take food to the office, church, club meetings, funerals, and other events, and have collected a lot of recipes through the years. I can tell you that every recipe in this book has been made by my grandmothers, mother, aunts, sisters, daughter, and myself.

Hope you enjoy the recipes.

Dedicated to:

Malvery Roberts Begley
and
Brenda Begley Baker

Mom and Brenda are two of the best cooks in my family, and they approved every recipe in this book.

Beverages & Appetizers

Mac & Linda Sibley
December 2016

Sweet Iced Tea

3 quarts water, give or take
2 cups sugar
4 quarts size tea bags

Bring water to a rolling boil, add sugar. Stir to dissolve. Add 4 tea bags. Stir. Let sit 20 minutes. Pour up into gallon jug or container. Fill the rest with cool water. Garnish with lemon or fresh mint.

Texas Sun Tea

3 family-sized tea bags
3 quarts cold water
Place tea bags in a 1-gallon glass jar and add cold water. Cap loosely and place in a sunny spot for 3 hours. Remove bags. Serve in large ice-filled glasses and garnish with lemon slices or sprigs of mint. So good!

Dove's Nest Orange Spiced Iced Tea

6 cups water
1 tea bag orange pekoe tea
2 tea bags Bigelow Constant Comment
Fresh orange slices
Bring 4 cups of the water to a boil in a saucepan. Add the tea bags; steep for 5 to 10 minutes. Stir in the remaining 2 cups water. Serve over ice with fresh orange slices. Yields 6 to 8 glasses.

Sassafras Tea

Gather young roots of sassafras or buy. Wash them in cold water. Scrape off the outer layer of bark and discard it. Bring the roots to a boil in water. To make a gallon of tea, boil 4 average size roots in a gallon of water for 15 to 20 minutes. Strain it. Sweetened with sugar or honey.
*Sassafras can be ordered from Amazon.

Soiree Punch

2- quart ginger ale
1- quart orange sherbet
Have ginger ale very cold. Pour 1 quart over sherbet in punch bowl ½ hour before serving. Add second quart when ready to serve. Makes 16 to 20 servings.

Fruit Slush

1 package unsweetened Kool-Aid
1 cup sugar
3 cups water
46 ounce can pineapple juice

Combine all ingredients and mix well. Place in freezer. Add 1 large bottle of ginger ale when ready to serve.

I use this for almost every party at our church. It's delicious and cheap. At Christmas I use red Kool-Aid. Lemon-Lime is good during the summer months and I usually add slices of lime in the punch bowl. I usually make at least 4 batches at one time.

Cranberry Wreath Punch

2 quarts cranberry juice
1 can (46 oz.) pineapple juice
1 cup lemon juice
2 quarts ginger ale
Ice

Chill all ingredients. Pour cranberry juice, pineapple juice, and lemon juice into a large punch bowl and stir. Add ginger ale and ice. Serve at once.

Dove's Nest Eggnog

1 half gallon Blue Bell Homemade Vanilla Ice Cream.
1 to 1-1/2 cups bourbon, or to taste
Freshly ground nutmeg

Soften the ice cream in a large punch bowl. Add the bourbon, stirring to blend. Sprinkle with nutmeg. Serve well chilled.

Café Au Lait

1-quart milk
1-pint strong hot coffee
¾ cup sugar

Place milk in a saucepan, allow to come to a boil, and immediately remove from heat. Add coffee and sugar, blend, and serve hot.

Extension Service Punch

10 cups sugar
5 cups water
24 ounces lemon juice concentrate
1 (46 ounces) cans grapefruit juice
1 (46 ounces) can orange juice
2 (46 ounces) cans pineapple juice
1-ounce almond extract
2- or 3-gallons water

Make a syrup of sugar and water. Then add the remaining ingredients. The larger the crowd, the more water added. This makes a lot of punch. I make this ahead and freeze; before party, let melt to slush.

Kentucky Punch Recipe

4 cups bourbon whiskey
1-1/2 cup lemonade concentrate
1-1/2 cups orange juice concentrate
1 cup lemon juice
8 cups lemon-lime soda

Thaw both concentrates but do not dilute. Then mix all the ingredients except soda in a large punch bowl and chill. When thoroughly chilled, add a block of ice in the bowl and stir in the soda. Serve in punch cups and garnish with slices of lemon, lime or orange. This punch makes approximately 30 servings.

Homemade Hot Chocolate

3 ½ cups sugar
2 ¼ cups cocoa
1 tablespoons table salt
Whole milk for serving

In a large bowl, combine sugar, cocoa, and salt, and whisk to combine well. Store the mixture in an airtight container.

For individual servings, pour 1 cup whole milk into a microwave-safe mug, and microwave on high just until hot. Add 2 tablespoons of cocoa mix and stir to dissolve. For a larger batch of cocoa, warm the milk in a saucepan set over medium-hot heat, taking care not to let the milk boil; as it warms, stir in 2 tablespoons of mix for each cup of milk.

My grandson, Korbin Thayer, and I enjoy hot chocolate any time of the year.

Frosty Wedding Punch

3-ounce package cherry gelatin
9 cups boiling water
4 cups sugar
4 cups water
2-46 ounces can pineapple juice
6 ounces frozen orange juice
4 teaspoon lemon juice
2 quarts ginger ale

Dissolve the gelatin in the boiling water in a large saucepan. In a separate saucepan boil the sugar and 4 cups water. Add the pineapple juice, orange juice, and lemon juice. Cool. Combine the gelatin and juice mixture. Pour into plastic containers and freeze. Set out about 3 hours before serving. Add the ginger ale just before serving.

The punch will be slushy. I have used this for several weddings. Really good tasting.

Tequila Lime Punch

2 cups cold water
1 ½ cup tequila
1 (6 ounce) can frozen pineapple-orange juice concentrate, thawed.
½ cup lime juice
2 tablespoons sugar
2 (28 ounce) bottles lemon-lime carbonated beverage, chilled
1 lime sliced
1 orange sliced

In a large punch bowl combine water, tequila, orange-pineapple concentrate, lime juice, and sugar. Slowly pour lemon-lime beverage down side of bowl. Stir punch gently with an up-and-down motion until mixed. Float the lime and orange slices atop punch in bowl. Serve over ice in punch cups. Makes 24 (1/2 cup) servings.

Hot Spicy Punch

4 cups (1 quart) apple juice
2 cups unsweetened pineapple juice
½ cup lemon juice
1 package (11 ounce) red hots
¼ teaspoon ground cloves
1 teaspoon cinnamon
2 cups water

Place all ingredients in a large pot or coffee urn. Heat until the red hots melt. Serve piping hot.

Old-Fashioned Lemonade

1 ½ cups sugar
½ cup boiling water
1 ½ cup fresh lemon juice
Grated peel of 1 lemon
5 cups cold water

In a large pitcher, add the sugar to the boiling water, stirring until dissolved. Add the lemon juice and lemon peel; mix well. Add the cold water, stirring until well-combined. Yields: 1 quart (4 to 6 servings)

Serve in tall glasses over ice and garnish with lemon slices. If you want to get festive, plan and make colorful ice cubes by dropping small wedges of lemon, green maraschino cherries, and strawberry halves into ice cubes trays, then filling with water and freezing. I like to freeze red maraschino cherries.

Betsy's Wassail

1-quart orange juice
1-quart pineapple juice
1-quart lemonade
1-gallon tea (sweet to taste)
24 whole cloves
6 cinnamon sticks (I use fresh Mexican Cinnamon Sticks)

Combine all ingredients and simmer for 10-15 minutes. Do not boil. Remove the cinnamon sticks and cloves. Serve hot. Makes 32 cups.

My friend, Betsy Tennison, makes this for the holidays. So good.

Aunt Janie's Tangy Vegetable Dip

½ cup water
3-ounce package lemon Jell-O
1 can tomato soup, undiluted
3 (8 ounce) package cream cheese
1 cup chopped green pepper
½ cup chopped onion
1 cup Miracle Whip
¾ cup chopped pecans

Heat water, tomato soup, lemon Jell-O and cream cheese and beat until smooth. (I use a hand mixer). Finely dice (use blender) green pepper and onion. Add Miracle Whip and chopped pecans. Mix all ingredients and chill.

Mac and I have been married a little over 50 years. I have made this dip for most of our married life. Aunt Janie Middleton Ralston would have family gatherings. She would make this dip. It was so good, so I asked for the recipe. I make this a lot.

Linda's Dip

1 can Ro-Tel tomatoes with chilies
1 can cream of mushroom soup
1 lb. sausage
1 lb. hamburger
2 lbs. Velveeta Cheese

Put Ro-Tel tomatoes in a crockpot. Add the mushroom soup and let this be heating while you cook the sausage and drain off fat and cook hamburger and drain off fat. Put sausage and hamburger in crockpot. Soften the Velveeta Cheese or melt before adding to the crockpot to speed up the melting process. Serve with chips.

This dip is delicious. I have made it hundreds of times for church events. You can use just one meat or spice it up with hot Ro-Tel.

Mexican Corn Dip

4 cans Fiesta whole kernel corn drained
2 (8-ounce) boxes cream cheese softened
1 small can chopped black olives
1 bunch green onions
Jalapenos to taste (*I use canned, 5-6 optional)
2 packages Fiesta Ranch Dip mix (dry mix)

Mix all ingredients together and refrigerate or serve immediately.

Sweet and Sour Party Meatballs

In a large crock pot add 2 pounds of frozen meatballs. Add 1 (12-ounce bottle chili sauce and 1 ½ cups grape jelly. Let simmer until hot. Then put a toothpick on each one and place on plate. I usually double the recipe. People really like them.

Sausage Stuffed Jalapenos

1-pound bulk pork sausage
1 (8-ounce) pkg. cream cheese
1 cup (4 ounce) shredded Parmesan cheese
22 large jalapeno peppers; halved lengthwise and seeded
Ranch salad dressing (opt.)

In a large skillet, cook the sausage over medium heat until no long pink; drain. In a small mixing bowl, combine the cream cheese and Parmesan cheese; fold in sausage. Spoon about 1 tablespoon into jalapeno half. Place in 2 ungreased 13x9x2-inch baking dishes. Bake, uncovered, age 425 degrees for 15 to 20 minutes, or until filling is lightly browned and bubbly. Serve with Ranch Dressing if desired. Yield: 44 appetizers.

Beth's Artichoke Dip

1 cup mayonnaise
2 cup artichoke hearts drained
¼ teaspoon garlic powder
1 teaspoon lemon juice
Ground pepper
1 cup grated Parmesan cheese

In mixing bowl, add all ingredients and blend with a mixer. Spread into a baking dish and heat at 350 degrees until bubbly.

Bourbon Frankfurters

1 cup bourbon
1 cut catsup
½ cup brown sugar
2 tablespoons minced onion
1/8 teaspoon Tabasco
1-pound cocktail franks cut in half crosswise

Combine all ingredients, except franks, in sauce pan. Simmer uncovered for 20 minutes, stirring frequently. Add franks and simmer an additional 15 minutes. This is an easy, but delicious dish using one of Kentucky's premier products.

Ed Leach's Hot Wieners

2 pints of white vinegar
5 packages of all meat wieners
2 (3.5 ounces) jars of red crushed peppers

Take wieners and cut in half. Place wieners in glass gallon jar. Take the 2 bottles of crushed peppers and pour into medium size cooking pan. Add approximately 2 cups of vinegar into the pan. Bring to complete boil. Pour this mixture onto wieners. Add vinegar until wieners are completely covered. Let set for 12 hours.
Great with crackers.

Ed Leach was for many years Police Chief for the City of Midlothian. He was from Jellico, Tennessee. He would bring these hot wieners to the office. Later I would make them. They never tasted as good as the ones that he made.

Dove's Nest Almond Bacon Cheddar Spread

12 strips of bacon, crisp-fried, crumbled
2 cups shredded cheddar cheese
½ cup chopped toasted almonds
¼ cup chopped green onions
½ cup mayonnaise
Dash of Tabasco sauce

Combine the bacon, cheese, almonds, green onion, mayonnaise and Tabasco sauce in a medium bowl, mix well.

Serve as a spread with crackers and fresh fruit or as a filling for sandwiches. This is the best!

Pimento Cheese Filling

½ pound cheddar cheese, shredded
¼ to ½ cup Dr. Pepper
1/8 teaspoon Tabasco
1/8 teaspoon salt (optional)
4 tablespoons sweet pickle relish
4-ounce canned pimento drained and chopped

Mix cheese, Dr. Pepper, Tabasco, and salt until light and fluffy. Fold in pickle relish and pimentos; chill before serving. Makes 1 pint and will make 12 to 15 sandwiches.

Chili-Cheese Dip

2 packages (8 ounce each) cream cheese, softened
2 cans (15 ounce each) chili with beans
1 bag (8 ounce) shredded cheese, nacho cheese works best

Spread cream cheese on the bottom of a square 8x8-inch baking dish. Cover evenly with chili. Sprinkle with shredded cheese. Microwave or bake until the cheese is melted bubbly.

Spinach Dip

1 (10 ounce) package frozen chopped spinach, thawed and drained
1 (16 ounce) carton sour cream
1 cup mayonnaise
1 package Knorr vegetable soup mix

In medium bowl, stir spinach, sour cream, mayonnaise and soup mix until mixed well. Cover, chill 2 hours to blend the flavors. Stir before serving.

Buffalo Chicken Dip

2 cups shredded (cooked) chicken breast
2 8-ounce packages cream cheese softened
1 cup Ranch dressing
¾ cup pepper sauce, such as Franks Red Hot
1 ½ cups shredded Cheddar Cheese
1 bunch celery cleaned and cut into 4-inch pieces
1 8-ounce chicken-flavored crackers

Heat chicken and hot sauce in a skillet over medium heat, until heated through. Stir in cream cheese and ranch dressing. Cook, stirring until well blended and warm. Mix in half of the shredded cheese and transfer the mixture to a slow cooker. Sprinkle the remaining cheese over and cook on low setting until hot and bubbly. It is best served hot with crackers and celery.

This is sister Brenda Begley Baker's recipe.

Bean Dip

32 ounces refried beans
2 cups shredded cheddar cheese
2 cups shredded Monterey Jack cheese
1 cup sour cream
8 ounces cream cheese
2 teaspoon taco seasoning

Place in Crock-Pot and cook until everything is melted together. Serve with tortilla chips.

Cindy's Tortilla Rolls

1 package burrito size flour tortillas
8-ounce sour cream
8-ounce soft cream cheese
1 small can chopped black olives
1 cup finely chopped green onion

Combine sour cream, cream cheese, olives and onions into mixing bowl. It's easier to mix if cream cheese is very soft. Mix all ingredients together well. Spread mixture over one entire side of each tortilla and roll. Put them all in the refrigerator ½ hour to 1 hour. Then cut into smaller pieces.

Cucumber Sandwiches

8 oz. cream cheese softened
3 tablespoons mayonnaise
1 pkg. Hidden Valley Ranch Mix
Party Rye bread
1 cucumber thinly sliced
Dill weed

Mix together cream cheese, mayonnaise, and ranch mix. Spread on party rye bread slice. Top each with a cucumber slice, then sprinkle with dill weed.

Tuna Sandwiches

1 can tuna
1 small can crushed pineapple
½ cup chopped pecans
1 (8 ounce) cream cheese
1 stalk celery finely chopped
2 hardboiled eggs
1 tablespoon sweet relish
1 tablespoon parsley

Mix all ingredients together. Spread between thin sliced bread and cut in strips of 2 or 4. Good for parties or women's club meetings.

Kentucky Benedictine Spread

1 (8 ounce) package cream cheese, softened
1 tablespoon mayonnaise
¼ cup sour cream
½ cup finely chopped cucumber
½ cup chopped green onion
½ teaspoon salt
¼ teaspoon black pepper
1/8 teaspoon dill weed
Pinch cayenne (optional)
1 to 2 drops green food coloring

Peel cucumber and split lengthwise down the middle. Take a spoon and remove the seeds before chopping. Mix together the cream cheese, mayonnaise, sour cream, salt, pepper, dill weed and cayenne with a mixer. Fold in the chopped cucumber, green onion and food coloring and mix with a spoon. Makes about 1 ½ cups. Enjoy with your favorite crackers or make into sandwiches.

Bev's Chicken Luncheon Salad

4 cups cooked chicken, chopped
2 cups celery, chopped
1 cup apples, chopped
1 cup pineapple chunks
½ teaspoon salt
1 ½ teaspoon curry
½ cup chopped almonds
1 cup mayonnaise
2 tablespoons lemon juice

Mix together in a large bowl and served with relish try and bran muffins. This recipe came from a lady in the Ellis County Republican Women. It is a recipe from England, as she was originally from there. I just serve it with fancy crackers.

Soups, Salads, & Vegetables

Bert Begley grinding corn

Potato Soup

3 medium potatoes peeled and cubed or sliced
½ onion, sliced thin
¼ pound butter
1 cup cream of celery soup, undiluted
1-2 cups milk
Salt to taste
Pepper to taste
Dash of garlic powder (optional)

Cover potatoes and onions with water and simmer until soft. Drain. Add butter to potatoes and mash, leaving some lumps. Add celery soup and milk. The amount of milk used, is determined by thickness desired. Heat until hot but do not boil.

Creamy Potato Soup

1-30 oz. bag frozen hash-browns potatoes cubed
2-14 oz. cans chicken broth
2-cans creamy celery soup
½ cup chopped onions
¼ teaspoons ground black pepper
1-8 oz. package cream cheese softened

In a slow cooker, combine potatoes, chicken broth, celery soup, onion, and pepper.
Cover and cook on low for 5-6 hours, if your potatoes are still in big chunks you need to cook it longer. They will start falling apart, when it is ready.

Add the cream cheese and cook 30 minutes or until cream cheese is melted, stirring occasionally, until combined. Top with cheese, bacon, or sliced green onions if desired.

I really like this soup. Easy and so good. I take it to church and other events.

Granny's Potato Soup

6 to 8 potatoes
1 large onion
3 tablespoons lard
2 ½ cup milk
1-quart tomato juice
1-quart water
Salt and pepper to taste
Cornstarch

Boil potatoes, onion and lard in water until done. Add tomato juice and milk, stirring constantly, to prevent sticking. Add salt and pepper to taste. Add cornstarch to thicken as desired.

This recipe came from cousin Marti Begley from Hazard, Perry County, Kentucky.

9E Ranch Cowboy Soup

2 pounds ground meat
1 chopped onion
1 can or fresh chopped green chili
1 can hominy or corn
2 cans pinto beans
3 cans chopped tomatoes (1 Ro-Tel if you like it hot)
1 pkg. dry taco mix
2 cups water

Brown the ground meat and onion together. Add the remaining ingredients. Mix all together and simmer 30 minutes.

Mary Rust's Bean Chowder

1 large can Great Northern White beans or 3 (15 oz.) cans
1 (28 oz.) can whole tomatoes
1 (28 oz.) can water
1 large potato cut into small squares
1 onion chopped
1 lb. pkg. good breakfast sausage
Salt and pepper to taste

Fry sausage with onion until done (pour off grease). Add rest of ingredients and slow-cook for 4 to 5 hours.

My sister, Avis Begley, gave me this recipe. It is so good and easy.

Cowboy Stew

1-1/2 pounds hamburger
1 medium chopped onion
Salt and pepper to taste
1 (4-ounces) can chopped green chilies or Ro-Tel
2 cups water
1 (16 ounces) can tomatoes or tomato sauce
4 medium peeled and diced potatoes
1 (15 ounces) Ranch-Style beans
1 (12 ounces) can corn
1 (10 ounces) can tomato soup

Brown beef and onion. Add salt and pepper. Drain beef and add remaining ingredients. Cook over medium heat for 1 hour.

This recipe came from my daughter's mother-in-law, Donna Thayer. Easy and very good.

Brenda's Cream of Broccoli Soup

1 medium onion chopped
6 tablespoon butter
6 tablespoon flour
4 cups water
4 chicken bouillon cubes
1 20 oz. bag chopped broccoli
1 cup milk
1 can cream of chicken soup
Salt and pepper to taste

Sauté onion in butter until tender. Add flour, stirring well. Gradually stir in water, bouillon, and broccoli. Cook over medium heat until broccoli is tender, stirring frequently. Reduce heat; stir in milk, cream of chicken soup, salt and pepper.

White Chili

3 cans white Navy beans
2 cans chicken broth
1 cup water
1-1/2 cup chopped onion
1 clove garlic
2 cups cooked/shredded chicken breast
1 can green chilies
1 tsp. oregano
½ tsp. red pepper flakes
1 cup cheddar cheese

Mix all ingredients except cheese. Simmer 45 minutes. Top individual bowls of chili with cheese.

My sister, Cynthia Begley Thompson, makes this recipe a lot. It is served many times in our Begley family.

Dog Bite Chili

1 tablespoon Spanish paprika
5 tablespoons chili powder
2 tablespoons Comino or cumin
1 teaspoon fresh garlic or 1 ½ granulated
½ teaspoon black pepper
½ teaspoon Mexican oregano or plain
1 can beef broth (1 ½ cups)
8-ounce tomato sauce
14-ounce can crushed tomatoes
1 medium bell pepper
3 pounds lean ground hamburger meat (90/10)
Medium onion
Canola oil for meat

Cook hamburger meat, onion, and bell pepper. Add beef broth, tomato sauce, and crushed tomatoes. Mix dry spices together and add 1/3 of spices to mixture. After the chili is about half done put another 1/3 of the spices in and mix well. Then just before done add the remaining spices. Let it simmer for 2 ½ to 3 hours. You can add 1 teaspoon cayenne if you want it hot.

This recipe is from cousin Malvery Roberts Powell. She said she got it from a military veteran from Rockport, Texas.

L.T. Felty's Chili

5 pounds lean beef coarsely ground
1-pound suet (raw fat of beef around the loins and kidneys)
1 medium onion
2 garlic pods pressed
1-ounce ground cumin seed
1-1/2 ounces Gebhardt's Chili Powder
1-pint water or tomato juice
1 tablespoon salt
Black or red pepper to taste

Place suet in bottom of a large, heavy pot and heat until suet is "melted out."
Add meat to suet and heat, stirring occasionally, until meat changes from pink to gray. This should be about 30 minutes. Add onion, garlic, cumin, chili powder, and water. Cook until meat is tender, 1 ½-2 hours. Add salt and black or red pepper, then eat and enjoy.

Mr. Felty was from Waxahachie and a very well-known chili head and "official expert chili cook advisor to the governor."

Chicken Corn Chowder

1 can cream of chicken soup
1 can cream of potato soup
1 ½ cup chicken broth
1 can Fiesta-style corn (do not drain)
1 cup milk
2 cups cooked chicken, diced
2 cups grated cheddar cheese

Put all ingredients except cheese into a large pot and heat. When to the boiling stage, lower heat and add cheese. Stir until cheese is melted. Serves 6.

Minestrone Soup

1-1 ½ pounds hamburger
2 can Ranch Style Beans
1 can corn or hominy
1 can Rotel
2 cans of Minestrone soup
1 chopped onion

Brown hamburger, drain, and add chopped onion. Cook until soft. Add beans, Rotel, tomatoes, and soup. Simmer 20-30 minutes. I got the recipe from cousin, Maudie Nave Roberts, Pond Creek, Oklahoma. I make it a lot.

Dove's Nest Tomato Basil Soup

1 cup chopped onion
5 cloves of garlic cut into halves
½ cup chopped bacon
3 (28-ounce) cans whole tomatoes
2 cups chick stock
2 teaspoons balsamic vinegar
1 cup whipping cream
½ cup chopped fresh basil
Salt and pepper to taste

Sauté the onion, garlic and bacon in the olive oil in a large saucepan until the bacon is cooked through and the vegetables are tender.

Add the tomatoes and chicken stock. Bring to a boil; remove from heat. Pour into a blender container. Process until the mixture is pureed. Stir in the vinegar, cream, basil, salt and pepper. Ladle into soup bowls. Serve immediately.

Senate Bean Soup

2 cups dried navy beans (about 1 pound)
12 cups water
1 ham bone
2 teaspoon salt
¼ teaspoon pepper
1 large chopped onion (about 1 cup)
2 stalks chopped celery (about 1 cup)
1 clove chopped finely garlic
2 ½ cups mashed, cooked potatoes

Heat beans and water to boiling in Dutch oven. Boil, uncovered, two minutes. Remove from heat. Cover and let stand one hour. Add ham bone. Heat to boiling; reduce heat. Cover and simmer about two hours or until beans are tender.
Stir in remaining ingredients. Cover and simmer one hour. Remove ham bone. Remove ham from bone and cut into bite-sized pieces. Stir into soup. Makes 12 servings with 95 calories per serving.

This recipe came from Mother. She enjoys this soup and makes it often.

Dove's Nest White Chili

2 tablespoons olive oil
1 medium onion chopped
3 cloves of garlic minced
2 ½ cups chopped fresh tomatoes, or 2 (10 ounce) cans tomatoes with green chilies, chopped
6 tomatillos chopped
1 medium jalapeno, seeded, minced
2 cups chicken stock
1 (7 ounce) can chopped green chilies
2 cups chopped cooked chicken
½ teaspoon oregano
½ teaspoon cumin
¼ cup (heaping) chopped cilantro
2 (19-ounce) cans cannellini or Great Northern beans
1 tablespoon fresh lime juice
Salt and pepper to taste
Sour Cream
Shredded Monterey Jack cheese
Fried tortilla strips

Heat the olive oil in a large stockpot over medium-high heat. Add the onion. Sauté for 3 to 5 minutes or until softened. Add the garlic. Cook until the tomatillos are tender, stirring occasionally.

Add the chicken stock, green chilies, chicken, oregano, cumin, cilantro, beans and lime juice. Cook until heated through, stirring frequently. Season with salt and pepper.

Ladle the chili into serving bowls. Serve garnished with a dollop of sour cream, shredded cheese and fried tortilla strips. Yield 8 to 10 servings.

Dove's Nest is a restaurant in Waxahachie, Texas. I must be honest and say I have never made White Chili. Mac doesn't like it. However, my sister, Brenda, makes this White Chili for her family and they really enjoy it.

Brenda's Spicy Vegetable Soup

1- pound ground chuck
1- cup chopped onion
2 cloves garlic minced
1 (30 ounce) jar chunky garden spaghetti sauce with mushrooms and peppers
1 (10 ½ ounce) can beef broth
2 cups water
1 cup sliced celery
1 teaspoon sugar
1 teaspoon salt
½ teaspoon pepper
1 (10 ounce) can diced tomatoes and green chilies
1 (16 ounce) package frozen mixed vegetables

Cook first 3 ingredients in a large Dutch oven over medium heat until meat is brown, stirring to crumble. Drain and return meat to pan. Add spaghetti sauce and next 6 ingredients. Bring to a boil; cover, reduce heat and simmer 20 minutes, stirring occasionally. Stir in tomatoes and mixed vegetables, return to boil. Cover, simmer 10-12 minutes. Great on a cold day "hearty" and so easy that we call this "Dump Soup". Just dump all the ingredients and simmer.

Mother with her brother, Charles Roberts

Mormon Potato Soup

2 large potatoes
2 large onions
8 slices back or ¼ pound salt pork
1 (1 pound) can tomatoes or 4 fresh tomatoes
1 teaspoon salt
1/8 teaspoon pepper
*I just use 1 quart of home canned tomatoes.

Peel potatoes and onions and cut into small pieces. Place into large saucepan and cover with water. Place over high heat. Bring to a boil and lower heat to gentle, rolling boil, about 10 minutes.

While vegetables are cooking, cut bacon or pork into small pieces. Cook in frying pan over medium heat until golden brown, but not too crisp. Remove bacon or pork with slotted spoon. Add to vegetables along with about a teaspoon of bacon fat. Add tomatoes (I just use 1 quart of home canned tomatoes) and simmer for about 10 minutes. Season with salt and pepper.

Mother got this recipe from Mormon Country in Melrose, Montana while she was visiting her brother.

Egg Salad

6 hard-cooked eggs chopped
¼ cup mayonnaise
1 teaspoon lemon juice
1 tsp. dried minced onion
Salt and pepper to taste
½ cup finely chopped celery

In bowl, combine the mayonnaise, lemon juice, onion, salt and pepper. Stir in eggs and celery. Cover and refrigerate. Yield 3 servings.

I really like egg salad sandwiches. I usually don't add the minced onion to mine. I like to add just a little pickle relish.

Old Fashion Bologna Salad

1-1/2-pound bologna, coarsely ground
4 hard-boiled eggs finely chopped
½ cup sweet pickle relish
1 tablespoon prepared mustard
1 cup mayonnaise
Salt and pepper to taste

Combine all the ingredients together. Cover and chill until ready to use. This makes about 1 quart of spread. Place your bologna salad on plain white sandwich bread.

I still enjoy a good bologna sandwich. The problem here in Texas it is hard to get good bologna. It just isn't the same as Kentucky bologna.

Frito Corn Salad

2 cans, whole kernel corn, drained
½ green bell peppers, chopped
½ red bell pepper, chopped
½ purple onion, chopped
1 cup mayonnaise or salad dressing

Mix all ingredients together and refrigerate. I refrigerate mine overnight. Before serving, add ¾ bag (9 ounces) Chili Cheese Fritos. This makes a lot so mix in a large bowl. This is such a pretty salad.

Bean Salad

1 can green beans
1 can kidney beans
1 can lima beans
1 can black olives
1 can chick peas
1 cup celery
1 cup onion
1 cup bell pepper
1 ½ cup white sugar
1 tsp. salt
¼ tsp. pepper
½ cup corn oil

Rinse all vegetables good. Chop celery. Slice onion and pepper thin. Then bring to boil sugar, white vinegar, corn oil, salt and pepper. Pour over vegetables. Set and chill to marinate. Keep refrigerated. Recipe from Aunt Ola Roberts Baker.

Apple Salad

4 medium Golden Delicious apples diced
4 medium Red Delicious apples diced
2 cups seedless green grapes halved
2 cups seedless red grapes halved
1 can (20 ounces) pineapple chunks, drained
1 can (11 ounces) mandarin oranges, drained

Dressing:
3 ounces cream cheese softened
½ cup sour cream
½ cup mayonnaise
½ cup sugar

In a large bowl, combine the first six ingredients. In a small bowl, beat dressing ingredients until smooth. Pour over fruit; toss gently to coat.

Timer's Cucumber Salad

2 medium cucumbers thinly sliced
1/3 cup cider vinegar
1/3 cup water
2 tablespoon sugar
½ tsp. salt
1/8 tsp. pepper
Fresh snipped dill or dried dill weed or finely chopped parsley

Taste cucumber. If it is bitter, sprinkle with salt and let stand for about 30 minutes. Then drain off accumulated liquid and proceed with recipe. Combine vinegar, water, sugar, salt, and pepper. Pour over cucumbers. If dried dill is to be used, add it at this time. Chill.

This is best if made early in the day and allowed to chill until serving time but making it close to meal time also works. Just before serving sprinkle with fresh dill or parsley.

I loved Timer Roberts. He was born in Leslie County, Kentucky and at an early age his parents moved to Pond Creek, Grant County, Oklahoma. He joined the military and traveled the world over. While in Europe he attended school to become a Le Cordon Bleu chef. After a long career in the military he retired and moved back to Pond Creek. I always enjoyed visiting him. He was a wonderful man, a great sense of humor.

Collier Road Pineapple Bake

1 #2 can crushed pineapple
½ cup milk
3 eggs beaten
Dash salt
1-pint sugar
½ cup margarine or butter

Boil all until thickened. Add 1-quart bread crumbs. Place in buttered baking dish. Sprinkle some butter and sugar on top. Bake at 350 degrees 40 to 45 minutes.

Mother said she made this for holidays when the family lived on Collier Road. It is good with ham.

Mother's Fruit Salad

20 ounce can pineapple chunks
2 large bananas, ¼ chunks
½ cup green grapes, sliced
½ cup red grapes, sliced
15-ounce mandarin oranges, drained
1 golden delicious apple diced and peel
1 red delicious apple diced with peel
½ cup sugar
2 tablespoon cornstarch
½ cup orange juice
1 tablespoon lemon juice
Kiwi on top, if you like, or any other fruit

Drain pineapple, reserve juice. Combine fruit in a large bowl. Set aside. In saucepan combine sugar and cornstarch. Add orange juice, lemon juice, and pineapple juice. Stir until smooth. Bring to boil. Add to the fruit and mix. I make this for Thanksgiving and Christmas.

Cherry Delight

1 can cherry pie filling
1 (20 ounce) can crushed pineapple, drained
1 can Eagle Brand milk
1 large container Cool Whip
1 cup chopped pecans
Coconut (if desired).

This is made for every Sibley family gathering and for funeral dinners. Korbin and his granddaddy, Mac, especially likes it.

Spring Salad

1 package (8 ounces) Cool Whip
1 box (3 ounces) Pistachio Pudding
¼ cup chopped nuts
1 (20 ounces) crushed pineapple
1 ½ cup mini-marshmallows

Mix all the ingredients. Chill.

Brenda's Wilted Lettuce Salad

6 ounces of slices bacon diced
¼ cup vinegar
2 tsp. sugar
2 bunches leaf lettuce, coarsely shredded
2 green onions with tops, chopped (about ½ cup)
¼ tsp. salt
1/8 tsp. pepper
2 Chopped boiled eggs

Place lettuce in bowl or on platter. Cook bacon in skillet until crisp, remove bacon from skillet, leave grease in skillet. Drain bacon on paper towel. Stir in vinegar and sugar in skillet with grease. Heat until hot; remove from heat. Pour hot dressing over lettuce. Toss until wilted. Top with onions and chopped boiled egg. Salt and pepper to taste.

Mother's ready to eat Wilted Lettuce

Helen Tucker's Broccoli Salad

½ cup white raisins (1/2 pound)
½ medium chopped purple onion
½ pound bacon, fried crisp, crumble
1 (8 oz.) can sliced water chestnuts, drained
1 head broccoli, broken into flowers
Mix first 5 ingredients together. Mix dressing well.

Dressing:
1 cup real mayonnaise
1 tablespoon vinegar
1/3 cup sugar

Mix and toss with salad. Refrigerate until served.

Oriental Cabbage Salad

1 small head cabbage chopped
1 grated carrot
2 bunches green onions chopped

Mix cabbage, carrots, and onions and chill just before you serve.

Add:
1 cup sunflower
1 cup silvered almonds
2 package chicken flavor Ramen noodles

Add dressing:
2 flavor packages from noodles
¾ cup oil
1/3 cup vinegar
½ cup sugar

Wild Raspberry Salad

1 (3 ounces) package raspberry Jell-O
1-pound cottage cheese
1 small package Cool Whip
1 cup crushed pineapple

Bring pineapple to a boil. Add Jell-O, stirring constantly until dissolved. Cook on low heat 2 minutes. Cool, then blend cottage cheese and Cool Whip. Add to cooled Jell-0. Keep in refrigerator until serving time.

Fruit Delight

1 8-ounce carton small curd cottage cheese
1 3-ounce package orange gelatin
1 8-ounce container frozen whipped topping, thawed
1 8-ounce can crushed pineapple, drained
1 8-ounce can Mandarin oranges, drained

Combine cottage cheese and dry orange gelatin. Add whipped topping and mix well. Fold in the pineapple and mandarin oranges until thoroughly blended. Chill and serve.

Thelma's Sour Cream Cranberry Salad

6 ounces raspberry gelatin
2 cups hot water
1 cup sour cream
1 can jelled cranberry
1 cup chopped pecans

Mix jelled cranberry and 1 cup boiling water in a blender or with a mixer until liquid is smooth. Dissolve 6 ounces raspberry gelatin in 1 cup boiling water. Add cranberry mixture and chopped pecans to gelatin. Put half the mixture in the bottom of the dish you will be serving it in. Chill until firm. Spread sour cream over top. Add second half of gelatin mixture over sour cream. Refrigerate until firm.

This recipe came from my sister, Velma Sizemore Julian. She said this was the recipe of Thelma Slusher Sizemore, her mother. She still makes it for her family.

Deviled Eggs

I take twelve or so hard-cooked eggs and cut them in half, lengthwise. Then remove yolks and mash with a fork in a bowl. I then add, to start, probably a half cup or so of mayonnaise, a couple tablespoons of mustard, and a half cup or so of sweet relish. I use my fork and mix well. Then add just a couple of tablespoons of pickle juice (any kind) that I might have in the refrigerator. If I have it, I add a little pimento. If the mix is not wet enough, I add more mayonnaise. Then I salt and pepper to taste. Spoon the egg yolk mixture into the egg whites. Sprinkle with paprika, if desired.

Hash Brown Casserole

1-10 oz. cream of mushroom soup
¾ cup sour cream
¾ cup milk
¾ cup melted butter
1 teaspoon seasoning salt
1 teaspoon black pepper
2 teaspoons garlic powder
¾ cup grated parmesan cheese, divided
2 cups grated cheddar cheese (more to top after baking, if desired)
1 small onion chopped
2-3 green onions chopped
1-2-pound frozen hash browns thawed

Set oven to 350 degrees. Butter a 13x9 inch casserole dish.

In a large bowl stir together the undiluted soup, milk, sour cream, melted butter, and ¼ cup parmesan cheese; whisk or mix until well combined.

Mix in the cheddar cheese, onions, and hash browns. Spread into prepared baking dish. Sprinkle with about ½ cup parmesan cheese.

Bake uncovered for 40 minutes or until hot and it bubbles.

I think this is better without the garlic powder. Also, Mac doesn't like the cheese on top.

If desired, sprinkle about 2 cups grated cheddar cheese on top and return to oven for 3 minutes to melt the cheese. Great recipe for big gatherings.

Dorothy's Potatoes

1 (2 lb.) pkg. frozen hash browns, thawed
1 (16 oz.) carton sour cream
1 can cream of chicken soup, undiluted
½ cup chopped onions
½ cup melted butter
1-1/2 tsp. salt
1 (8 oz.) pkg. sharp Cheddar Cheese

Mix all ingredients in 9x13-inch baking dish (don't cover). Bake at 325 degrees for 1 hour.

This recipe was from my dear cousin, Dorothy Roberts Ouellette. I have made this dish a lot.

Mountain Green Beans and Taters

2 pounds green beans
¼ pound salt pork
½ teaspoon salt, plus more for seasonings
16 golf-ball size new potatoes

Prepared the beans by removing the strings and snapping them into pieces about 1 inch long. Place the beans in a large lidded pot and add enough water to just cover them. Nestle the piece of salt pork in the center of the beans. Add the ½ teaspoon salt to the water. Bring the water to a boil on high heat. Reduce the heat to a lively simmer, cover the pot and cook until beans (not the green pods, but the beans themselves) are tender. This takes about 1 hour, and you may need to add water to keep the beans from cooking dry. Check the pot often.

Taste the broth and the beans and add additional salt if needed. Place the potatoes in the pot, pushing them down into the broth. Cover and simmer for 20 or 30 minutes, until the potatoes are tender enough to break apart easily. Remove the salt pork and serve.

Sibley Family Reunion Baked Beans

1 lb. can pork and beans
½ cup brown sugar
½ cup catsup
½ cup cane syrup
2 tsp. prepared mustard
1/8 tsp. ginger
1 small onion chopped
Dash of pepper
2 strips bacon

Mix together and place in 375-degree oven for 45 minutes.

Kentucky Fried Corn

5 ears fresh corn-cut off cob
Salt and pepper to taste
2 teaspoons sugar
3 tablespoon flour
3 tablespoons bacon grease

Mix all ingredients, except bacon grease. Melt grease in large frying pan. Add corn mixture and simmer on low heat for about 40 minutes. Stirring a few times to make sure it doesn't stick.

Be sure to get the corn scraped good and get all the "milk" or juice off the cob.

Corn Pudding

1 can whole kernel corn
1 can cream style corn
1 cup sour cream
2 eggs, slightly beaten
1 stick melted butter
1 box Jiffy Corn Bread mix

Mix all together. Bake at 350 degrees 40 minutes or until done.

Fried Cabbage

1 head cabbage chopped
4 teaspoons lard or other shortening
Bacon crumbled
Salt and pepper to taste

Bring about an inch of water in a large frying pan to boil. Add the lard and cabbage. If the cabbage head is large; just cut in half. Salt and pepper to taste. Cover and simmer for about 25 to 30 minutes. Take cover off and let the cabbage brown to your liking. Crumble bacon over cabbage.

Greens

Any vegetable greens (collard greens, turnip green, kale, and mustard greens), strip of salt pork, ½ inch by 3-inch, salt and water.

Pick over the leaves of the greens and remove any spotted parts or discolored leaves and stems. Wash leaves carefully and thoroughly until free of sand and soil. The turnip greens will have edible white roots-trim the stem top and root part off each and wash. Slice and cut into quarters and cook with leaves. Place the washed leaves in a large sauce pan. Add a little cool water and the salt pork. Then salt to taste. Bring to a boil, reduce heat, and simmer until just tender, 20-30 minutes. Serve with vinegar.

Calabacitas (Skillet Squash)

5 cubed small summer squash
1 diced large onion
2 roasted peeled green chilies or about 1 small can dice green chilies
1 tablespoon shortening or oil
¼ cup shredded longhorn cheese

Sauté onion in shortening or oil until soft. Add squash and stir until almost tender. Add chilies; simmer briefly. Sprinkle on cheese and stir until melted.

Leather Breeches Beans (Shuck Beans)

Mama Avis Napier Roberts would string the green beans. She would fill a long needle with a long strong thread, filling from knot end to needle. She would never break up the beans as she thought that would make the beans tough. She would string the entire bean instead. I am sure that is how she was taught by her mother, Mary Sizemore Napier. The string would be hung by one end in the warm air, but not in direct sunlight and sometimes behind the wood burning stove. She would let them remain hanging until the beans became dry. The beans would be stored in a pillow case or jars. Black or red pepper would be put in with the beans to keep out bugs.

Grandmother Ida White Begley would not string up her beans. She would remove the strings and break the beans in the same manner as for cooking. She would then spread the beans thinly on a sheet and place them in the sun on a big rock. I can still remember seeing the beans on that rock drying. Each day before the dew fell the sheet was brought in then taken back out each morning after the sun rose. It usually took seven to ten days to dry the beans. After the beans were dry, they were placed in jars and stored in the cellar.

When she wanted a mess of beans for a meal, she took the gallon jar from the cellar and poured out as many as she wanted. I remember helping her do this on many occasions. Since they were already prepared for cooking, she put them in a good-sized pot and covered them with water. She would bring to a boil for about 5 minutes. Then drain water and wash. Cover with water again and added fat back (salt pork) and cook gently until done.

Favorite Green Beans

1 pound of frozen green beans-rinse under hot water in colander for several minutes to partial thaw then
1/2 pound of bacon-cooked until crisp and chopped
1/2 cup butter
1/2 tablespoon fresh minced garlic
1/2 cup brown sugar
1 Tablespoon soy sauce

Place green beans in baking dish.

Add butter, garlic, brown sugar, and soy sauce in small sauce pan. Bring to boil.
Pour mixture over green beans and cover. Marinate overnight in refrigerator. Bake at 350 degrees for approximately 30-35 minutes or until hot. This recipe is easily doubled. You can adjust measurement to your liking.

My nephew, Jimmy, brings them to Thanksgiving dinner and other Sibley events. I have also made this for catering events.

Turnip Greens with Turnips

2 pounds turnip greens
1 teaspoon sugar
8 slices bacon
¼ tsp. salt
3 medium turnips peeled and sliced

Wash turnip greens thoroughly, tear or cut into bite sized pieces. Combine greens and bacon in a Dutch oven; cover with water and bring to a boil. Cover, reduce heat, and simmer 20 minutes. Stir in turnips, sugar, salt and pepper. Cover and cook an additional 30 minutes or until turnips are tender.

Corn Pudding

3 eggs
3 tablespoon flour
¼ cup sugar
1 ½ cup milk
1 can whole kernel corn, drained
1 can cream style corn
½ tsp. salt
½ stick butter

Combine eggs, flour and sugar, beat well. Add milk, corn and salt. Mix well. Melt butter in baking dish. Add corn mixture to hot butter. Bake at 375 degrees for 45-60 minutes or until firm. Serves 8-10.

This recipe came from cousin Wilma Jean Holland Hollen.

Country Seasoned Greens

Any vegetable greens (collard greens, turnip greens, kale, and mustard greens), strip of salt pork, ½ inch by 3-inch, salt and pepper.

Pick over the leaves of the greens and remove any spotted parts or discolored leaves and stems. Wash leaves carefully and thoroughly until free of sand and soil. The turnip greens will have edible white roots-trim the stem top and root part off of each and wash.

Slice and cut into quarters and cook with leaves. Place the washed leaves in a fairly large sauce pan. Add a little cool water and the salt pork. Then salt to taste. Bring to a boil, reduce heat, and simmer until just tender, 20-30 minutes. Serve with vinegar.

This recipe came from cousin Wilma Jean Holland Hollen.

Hickory Chickens or Morel Mushrooms

2 eggs
Salt water
2 cups cornmeal
1 cup milk
1 cup flour
Pepper to taste
Grease

Cut hickory chickens in half if medium-sized to big. Place in salt water and let soak a few hours in salt water to kill the bugs and clean them. Drain off the water. Melt grease in skillet. Let it get hot before placing the hickory chickens in.

To prepare the hickory chickens before frying, mix together the eggs and milk and set aside. In another bowl mix flour and cornmeal together. Take the hickory chickens and dip into the egg and milk mixture. Then dip into the flour and cornmeal mixture. Then place in the hot grease and pepper. Let fry until golden brown. Wonderful if you can get the mushrooms. So good with a little Ranch dressing.

Fried Cucumbers

3 or 4 large cucumbers
1 beaten egg
1 cup cornmeal
Cooking oil

In large skillet heat oil, about ½ cup. While oil is heating, peel cucumbers and slice lengthwise like French fries. Dip cucumber sticks in bowl of beaten egg, then dip in cornmeal. Layer cucumbers in skillet and fry for a few minutes then turn on other side. Drain on paper towel. Can salt if you like. Recipe came from cousin Wanda Holland.

Aunt Mae's Fried Potatoes

¼ cup shortening
4 cups raw, pared potatoes slice 1/8 inch thick
Salt and pepper to taste.

Melt shortening in heavy skillet (cast iron is best) over high heat. Add potatoes, salt and pepper. Cover and fry 10 minutes, stirring occasionally. Reduce heat until potatoes seem done, still stirring often. Uncover and fry about fifteen minutes, or until golden brown, stirring frequently. Serves 4. You can add 1 cup sliced onions to potatoes and fry as above.

Aunt Mae Bowling Roberts lived on T Street in Manchester, Kentucky. She always wanted to cook for us when we came to visit.

Mother's Fried Turnips

Peel and slice turnips. Place into skillet that has a little bacon fat, butter or oil. Add a little water and sprinkle with salt, pepper and sugar. Put lid on skillet, turn occasionally. Fry until brown.

Polk Sallet Greens

In the spring after all the danger of frost has passed, go out into the fields and woods and pick a mess of poke. You don't want it to get too big. Wash the greens thoroughly, then put in a kettle and cover with water, parboil for a few minutes, pour this water off, then add fresh water (not too much, just cover the poke).

Cook until tender (only takes a little while). Drain water off poke, put in frying pan where you have fried a few slices of bacon. Het thoroughly and cook down. Serve. Have a little vinegar in a cup to pour over greens, if desired.

Peggy's Rice

Heat together:
1 can French Onion soup
½ stick butter
1 cup water
Add:
1 cup rice
1 can mushrooms

Bake in casserole at 350 degrees for 45 minutes.

Mary Roberts' Soup Beans

1-pound pinto beans
1-pound white Great Northern beans
3 tablespoons lard
1 small piece salt pork or ham
Salt to taste

Place beans in a large cooker and add enough water to cover beans. Heat to boiling. Remove from heat and cover. Soak beans in the hot water for about 3 hours. Then wash beans in a couple rinses of water. Add enough water to cover beans. Add salt, lard and salt pork or ham. Cook about 2 hours on low heat. Keep plenty of water in beans.

Slow-Cooker Macaroni and Cheese

8 ounces elbow macaroni
3 cups (12 ounces) shredded sharp cheddar cheese
1 (12 ounces) can evaporated milk
1 ½ cups milk
2 eggs lightly beaten
1 teaspoon salt
¼ teaspoon pepper
1 cup (4 ounces) shredded sharp cheddar cheese
4 slices American cheese

Prepare the pasta according to the package directions. Drain. Mix the cooked pasta, 3 cups cheddar cheese, the evaporated milk, milk, eggs, salt and pepper in a greased slow cooker. Sprinkle with 1 cup cheddar and arrange the American cheese on top. Cook, covered on low for 3 to 4 hours. Do not remove the lid or stir while cooking.

Chuck Wagon Beans

4 cups pinto beans
1-pound salt pork or ham hocks
2 medium onions chopped
2 tablespoons sugar
3 teaspoons chili powder
6 ounces tomato paste
Salt to taste

Wash beans and soak overnight. Drain, place in a large kettle or Dutch oven and cover with water. Add remaining ingredients, except for salt. Simmer 3-4 hours, stirring occasionally. Add salt to taste and more water if needed. Cook another hour, or until beans are tender.

Pan Fried Apples

1 or 2 tablespoon vegetable shortening
4 cups sliced apples
1 cup sugar *depending on type of apple, may need less or more

Heat shortening in iron skillet and add apples. Stir in sugar, really to taste. Cover and cook for about five minutes or so until the sugar liquifies. Remove lid and fry, stirring occasionally, until apples are tender, and the liquid is cooked away.

Isabelle's Potato Cakes

2 cup mashed potatoes
1 cup bread crumbs
1 small onion grated
2 beaten eggs
½ cup rich milk
Salt and pepper to taste
Corn meal

Combine all ingredients, except corn meal and shape into cakes. Roll each in corn meal. Brown on both sides in hot bacon fat.

Isabelle Roberts Begley is one of the best cooks in our family.

My Kentucky Soup Beans

Remove bad beans and rocks from 1 pound of pinto beans. After sorting through rinse, the beans well. Place in a large heavy pot and cover with water, about 2 inches or so. Let soak overnight or at least let them soak for an hour or so before cooking.

After the beans have soaked, drain the water off. Remove the beans from pot. To the pot add a couple of tablespoons of lard and a ½ onion. Sauté a few minutes; add fresh water to cover beans. Add salt pork or ham. Turn onto high heat until the beans come to a boil. I usually allow them to boil for about 20-30 minutes. Add water, if needed. Then turn down the heat to a medium heat, cover, and allow to simmer for 2 to 3 hours, stirring occasionally. Some people do not add the salt until they are done. I add the salt early and like to add paprika and black pepper.

Mac will eat soup beans, but not his favorite beans. I must have them, of course, you must make cornbread. One of my favorite meals that I can remember Mother making was soup beans, fried potatoes, onions, and cornbread.

Aunt Opal's Potato Salad

Boil about 8 to 10 potatoes and cook until fork tender. Drain the water and let them cool. Boil 6-8 eggs. In a dish pan, chop 2 onions (or to taste) and 3 or 4 pickles. Peel and cut the potatoes and eggs up and add to the onions and pickles. Mix in 1 tablespoon of mustard and 1 cup mayonnaise. Salt and pepper to taste.

This recipe is from Aunt Opal Roberts Davidson and is one of the best. Mother makes her potato salad about the same but will sometimes add a little pickle juice. She also uses a small jar of drained pimento. I use this recipe but use pickle relish instead of pickles and add the small jar of drained pimento. I sprinkle paprika on top of the potato salad.

Orange Peas Amandine

1 tablespoon butter
2 tablespoons orange marmalade
1 (15 ounce) can small early peas, drained
1/3 cup sliced almonds, toasted

To toast almonds, heat oven to 350 degrees. Spread almonds on cookie sheet. Bake at 350 degrees for 5 to 7 minutes until light golden brown. Melt butter in medium saucepan. Add orange marmalade. Stir until blended. Gently stir in peas and almonds. Heat through.

I found this recipe in a cookbook that I purchased at Red Bird Mission. It came from Rebecca Smallwood, Beverly, Clay County, Kentucky.

Mildred Roberts' Sweet Potato Balls

1 large can sweet potatoes
1 cup brown sugar
1 small can crush pineapple drained
Large marshmallows
Coconut
½ tsp. cinnamon

Mix sweet potatoes, sugar, pineapple, and cinnamon. Take a marshmallow and put some sweet potato mixture around. Make a ball. Make sure the marshmallow is covered. Put coconut on wax paper and roll ball in it. Butter a baking pan. Bake at 325 degrees for 20 minutes and coconut is a little brown.

Baked Cushaw Squash

Cushaw Squash
Brown sugar
Butter

Wash and clean Cushaw and cut into serving pieces. Sprinkle with brown sugar and spread with butter. Bake at 350 degrees until tender. Delicious with country ham.

Corn Vegetable Medley

1 can corn soup
½ cup milk
1 bag carrots, cauliflower, and broccoli
½ cup shredded Cheddar cheese

In saucepan, heat soup, and milk to boiling. Don't burn; stir in vegetables. Return to boil; turn to low heat for 20 minutes. Vegetables should be tender in 20 minutes. Stir in cheese; let melt.

Sour Cream Green Bean Casserole

1 chopped onion
¼ cup butter
1 tablespoon flour
1 cup sour cream
2 cans French cut green beans-drained
¼ teaspoon salt
Dash pepper
Sauté onion and butter. Add flour. When mixture is cool add sour cream. Add other ingredients and mix well. Place in buttered casserole.
Topping:
¼ pound grated swiss cheese
¼ cup corn flake crumbs
2 tablespoon melted butter
¼ cup slivered almonds (optional)

Mix together and spread over top of beans. Bake at 350 degrees for 35-40 minutes.
Recipe from sister, Velma Sizemore Julian.

Brenda's Oven-Baked Brandied Cranberries

1-pound cranberries (thawed, if frozen)
2 cups sugar
1 tablespoon orange zest (from 1 orange)
Kosher salt
¼ cup brandy, Grand Marnier or another orange-flavored liqueur

1. Heat oven to 350 degrees. Place the cranberries in a 9x13-inch or 3-quart baking dish. Add the sugar, zest and a pinch of salt; stir to combine.

2. Cover with foil and bake for 30 minutes, then uncover, stir and continue cooking, uncovered, until bubbling and slightly thickened, about 10 minutes.

3. Stir in the brandy and let sit for at least 10 minutes before serving. Makes 2 cups.

Meat & Main Dishes

Jim Roberts & Bert Begley

Chuck Pot Coca Cola Roast

1 beef roast
1 can cream of mushroom soup
1 pkg. dry onion soup mix
1- 12 oz. can Coke
Red potatoes halved
Carrots cut in chunks

Place beef in crock-pot and top with dry soup mix. Place vegetables around roast. Mix together the cream of mushroom soup and the coke in a bowl and pour over roast.

Set crock-pot on low, cook for 6-8 hours. The longer you cook, the more tender the meat becomes.

Crock-Pot Beef Tips

2 pounds stew meat
1 can Cream of Mushroom Soup
1 packet brown gravy mix
1 packet Lipton dry onion soup mix
1 small can mushrooms
1 cup water

Mix all ingredients and pour over the meat, set to low for the day. Served over potatoes, noodles, or rice.

Salmon Patties

1 can pink salmon
2 eggs, beaten
1 teaspoon of lemon juice
½ cup minced onion
1 teaspoon pepper
Saltine crackers
Cooking oil

Empty one can (14-3/4 ounces) of salmon, with juice, into a mixing bowl; removing the bones. Add the eggs and lemon juice and stir well. Stir in onion, pepper and crushed saltine crackers. Mix well and then form into patties about one inch thick. Set the patties aside on a plate for about five minutes. In a large frying pan heat ½ inch cooking oil to medium to high temperature. When oil is hot, place the patties in the pan and cook 4-5 minutes per side until brown.

Chicken Tetrazzini/Spaghetti

Cook one whole chicken until tender, reserving chicken broth. *I add chopped celery and chopped onion sautéed in butter. In fact, I use the same large pot and then add my chicken. I usually buy about 2-1/2 or 3 pounds of chicken breast to cook.

When the chicken is done, I remove it and use the same broth to cook 32 oz. of spaghetti. When spaghetti is done, do not drain-add 2 cans cream of mushrooms soup, 2 cans cream of chicken soup, and one can Rotel chopped tomatoes w/green chilies. Add chopped chicken and salt and pepper to taste.
Chop one (1) pound of Velveeta Cheese and mix well with above mixture.

Original recipe said to place in large casseroles (usually makes 2) and bake at 350 degrees until hot and bubbly. But I use my large crock pot and it works well. This feeds 20 people.

Crock Pot Roast

1- 4-5 pounds beef roast
1-1¼ oz. package brown gravy mix, dry
1-1 ¼ oz. package dried Italian Salad Dressing mix
½ cup water

1. Place roast in crock pot.
2. Mix dried mixes together in bowl and sprinkle over roast.
3. Pour over water around the roast.
4. Cook on low for 7-9 hours.

This is the recipe I usually use when making a beef roast. I usually just put this in a roasting pan. I add carrots, onions, and potatoes. I will do this early Sunday morning before Sunday School and church. I will put it on about 250 degrees and let it bake until we get home. I will add a salad and rolls and the meal is finished. I always invite the kids. They enjoy this meal.

Fried Chicken Livers

1-pound chicken livers
1 cup buttermilk
2 cups self-rising flour
1 tablespoon salt
2 tsp. black pepper

Soak livers in buttermilk for 5 minutes. Combine flour, salt, and pepper in a dish. Take livers and dredge each in flour and transfer to a plate. Pour at least 1- inch Crisco or lard into a cast-iron skillet. Heat to 340 degrees. Fry livers in batches into golden brown. Transfer to platter and sprinkle with sea salt.

Aunt Ola's Chicken Gizzards with Gravy

Trim excess fat and gristle from chicken gizzards. Rinse under cold running water. Place gizzards in a pressure cooker and cover with water. Cook in pressure cooker for about 45 minutes. In a pint jar add 1 cup flour and then fill pint jar with milk. Shake milk and flour until mixed well. When chicken gizzards are done pour in flour and milk mixture, stirring constantly until the mixture thickens. Then ready to serve.

Fried Chicken Gizzards

1 1/2 pounds chicken gizzards
1/2 cup all-purpose flour
1 1/2 tablespoons seasoned salt
1 1/2 teaspoons ground black pepper
1 1/2 teaspoons garlic powder (optional)
2 cups vegetable oil for frying

Trim excess fat and gristle from chicken gizzards. Rinse under cold running water.
Place gizzards in a pot of cold water. Bring water and gizzards to a rolling boil; continue to boil for about 15 minutes. Strain gizzards using a colander. Allow to cool. Meanwhile, combine the flour, seasoned salt, pepper, and garlic powder in a plastic bag. Shake well to combine.

Preheat vegetable oil in a skillet with a lid over medium-high heat to 375 degrees.

Thoroughly coat gizzards with flour mixture and shake off excess. Gently lay the coated gizzards in the hot oil. Cook until brown. Reduce heat to medium; cover skillet with lid and cook another 10 minutes. Remove to paper towels to drain.

Mac is a retired Dallas Police Officer. He worked most of his thirty-three-year career in Southeast Dallas, which is mostly a black population. Mac enjoyed eating at the restaurant, Henderson's Honey Fried Chicken. He really likes chicken gizzards. (Not me). He would go by there and for $1.50 buy about 20 gizzards and about a quarter pound of hot greasy delicious French fries. It was one of his favorite meals!

Deb's Dang Tacos

1-pound lean ground beef
1 onion, chopped in small pieces
Olive oil
4 Roma tomatoes, diced and place in refrigerator
½ head of thinly shredded ice berg lettuce, place in refrigerator
1 package Soft Corn tortillas
1 package of Mexican blend shredded cheese
Salt and pepper to taste

Tortilla Preparation:

In small sauce pan, add enough olive oil to coat the bottom of the pan, heat olive oil on medium/medium high heat. Using tongs, place a single corn tortilla and cook for about three seconds on each side then place tortilla on a paper towel to drain access oil. Repeat this process for desired number of tacos.

Taco meat preparation:

In a 10- or 12-inch skillet on medium heat, add 2 tablespoons of olive oil. When olive oil is hot, add diced onions and cook until almost clear. Add ground beef, salt, and pepper to taste. Stir frequently and cook until beef is done. Drain taco meat mixture.

On a dinner plate build 2 or 3 tacos per person. Corn tortilla, then meat, then chilled shredded lettuce, chilled diced tomatoes, and shredded cheese.

This recipe is a family favorite! I would typically make them on Taco Tuesday for my sons. It is also great for family/friend gatherings. No one ever asked for salsa or guacamole but can certainly be added.

If there were leftovers, I would assemble the tacos and place them in zip lock bags to reheat later.

Recipe from cousin Debi Black Vandiver.

Belizean Stew Chicken

1 whole chicken cut up with skin off
1 teaspoon cumin
2 teaspoons paprika
1 teaspoon dried thyme
1 small chopped onion
1-1/2 teaspoon black pepper
1 teaspoon Season-All
1 teaspoon garlic powder
1 teaspoon oregano
½ cup green bell pepper, chopped

Wash chicken with lime juice. In a large bowl, marinate chicken with spice, onion and bell pepper for about 45 minutes. Heat 2 tablespoons of oil in a large pot on medium heat and then add chicken and brown on both sides. After the chicken is brown, add the remaining marinade sauce along with onion, pepper, and a glass of water. Cover and let simmer for 45 minutes to 1 hour. Taste for flavor and adjust seasoning as needed. Serve with rice and beans, coleslaw, and fried plantain for a taste of one of Belize's most popular lunches.

This recipe came from Aunt Dorla Roberts. I visited Belize and really liked the food. They have wonderful chicken dishes.

Kentucky Fried Catfish

2 pounds skinned dressed catfish
Salt to taste
2 cups buttermilk
2 cups yellow cornmeal
Shortening

Cut the catfish into serving pieces and salt. Dip the catfish into the buttermilk and then roll in cornmeal. Fry fish until golden brown in hot shortening in a heavy skillet. Drain on paper towels before serving. I always use my iron skillet.

Fried Pork Liver and Onions

Wash the liver well and then salt and pepper. Roll in a mixture of cornmeal and flour. Mother says a lot of times she would just use flour. Fry in hot grease. Remove liver from the pan when browned and replace with onions. Let onions cook until brown then put the liver back into the pan on top of onions. Cover and simmer for twenty minutes.

Neck Bones

4 pounds pork neck bones
3 tablespoons lard
Salt and pepper
Large onion
Sage or flour optional

Wash the neck bones in warm water, drain, and dry. Then season with lard, salt, and pepper. Cover with water and add half of a large onion. Some people will add just a little sage, but Mother cannot remember Mama using sage, so she never does. The neck bones are covered and simmered for one hour until meat is almost done. Sometimes flour is added to the broth to thicken.

Mother still makes neck bones. I honestly only eat them when I am home with her. I am not a fan.

Fried Squirrel with Gravy

Clean the young squirrel thoroughly, disjoint it, and cut the back into two pieces. Put in a large glass container with salt water and soak overnight in the refrigerator.

When ready to cook, drain, and dry the pieces and remove any loose membrane, roll in flour that has been seasoned with salt and pepper. Heat oil or lard (not vegetable shortening) in a heavy skillet. Brown the pieces, turning once. Cover the skillet and cook about 30 minutes longer.

Remove from the skillet, pouring off all but three tablespoons of fat. Add two tablespoons seasoned flour and stir. When the flour becomes brown, stir in equal parts of milk and water and cook; stirring constantly until thick.

Squirrel and Dumplings

Cut up two or three squirrels. Wash the meat well and be sure all hair and shots have been removed. Place squirrels in water with a couple of tablespoons of lard and boil until tender.

Dumplings:
2 cups flour
1 egg
1 teaspoon salt
¾ cup of squirrel broth

Combine flour, egg, salt and broth. Roll on floured dough board until thin. Cut in strips 1 ½ to 2 inches long. Return to boiling broth and add black pepper. Cool uncovered for 10 minutes.

Fried Pork Chops

6 to 8 pork chops
Salt and pepper
1 or 1-1/2 cups flour
Lard or oil

Put the flour, salt, and pepper in a paper bag. Put a couple of pork chops in, at a time, and shake the bag well. Place the breaded pork chops in the hot lard and fry about 5 to 10 minutes on each side. Turn the chops as needed not to burn. Place on paper towels to drain.

Nancy's Sloppy Joes

2 pounds ground beef
1 large chopped onion
½ green diced pepper
1 tsp. salt
¼ cup sugar
2 tablespoon vinegar
1 tsp. dry mustard
1 ½ cup catsup

Brown meat. Add green pepper and onions. Add catsup, salt, vinegar, and dry mustard. Mix and simmer until thickened, about 1 hour. Serve on hamburger rolls.

Nancy Deisher Sibley was my sister-in-law. I still use this recipe as it is easy and my family like it.

Brenda's Chicken and Dumplings

About 3 cups cooked chicken
8 cups chicken broth
3 cups flour
2 tablespoon Crisco
½ teaspoon baking powder
Salt to taste
About a cup of chicken broth that is cooled, maybe a bit less

1. In a bowl, combine the flour, baking powder, and salt. Cut the Crisco into the dry ingredients with a fork or pastry blend.
2. Add broth a little at a time until soft dough is formed. Gently knead a couple times and from a ball.
3. Heavily flour a work surface. You will need a rolling pin and something to cut the dumplings with. I like to use a pizza cutter.
4. Roll the dough out think with a heavily floured rolling pin. Dip your cutter in flour and cut the dumplings in squares.
5. Use a floured spatula to put them on a heavily floured plate. Just keep flouring between the layers of dumplings.
6. To cook them, bring the broth to a boil. Drop the dumplings in one at a time, shake pot to stir or gently push down with spoon. It takes about 20 minutes to cook until tender.
7. Add the cooked chicken to the pot and you are done.

Mother, Malvery Roberts Begley, making Chicken & Dumplings

Cheyenne River Ribs

3 pounds pork or beef ribs
1 large chopped onion
½ cup water
¼ cup vinegar
Black pepper to taste
2 tablespoon brown sugar
1 tablespoon Worcestershire sauce
1 tablespoon dry mustard
1 tsp. salt
1 tsp. paprika

Arrange ribs in a single layer in a large shallow casserole dish. Bake in 350-degree oven for 1 hour. Skim off fat. Combine remaining ingredients in a saucepan and simmer for 30 minutes. Pour over ribs and cook for 1 to 1-1/2 hours, or until meat is tender.

I went to Alberta, Canada and bought a cookbook. This recipe was in it. It was from the Cheyenne River Ranch in Douglas, Wyoming. I made it mine.

Mrs. Duvall's Chicken Casserole

1 cup cooked chopped chicken
½ cup uncooked rice
1 can cream of chicken soup
1 small diced onion
½ cup diced celery
1 small jar pimentos
1 cup grated cheese

Cook rice and set aside. Sauté onion and celery. Mix first 6 ingredients together. Put in casserole. Add grated cheese on top. Cook until bubbly at 350 degrees.

Fried Bologna Sandwich

2 slices beef bologna per sandwich
2 tablespoons butter
2 pieces of white bread

Cut slits in the bologna and fry until brown on each side. In another skillet place a couple of tablespoons of butter to melt. Place the bread in the skillet and start browning on both sides. Add the bologna between the bread and let the sandwich become a nice brown on each side. Be careful and do not let it burn. If you want cheese you can add it to the sandwich. What can be better than a good fried bologna sandwich?

Aunt Quata Sibley's Meat Loaf

1 egg slightly beaten
¾ cup bread crumbs
2 tablespoon chopped onion
2 tablespoon chopped green pepper
1 tsp. Worcestershire Sauce
½ cup milk
1 ½ pound ground meat
¼ tsp. black pepper
2 tsp. sale
¼ cup catsup

Combine egg, onion, and bread crumbs and let soak 10 minutes. Add remaining ingredients and mix well. Place in greased dish. Bake at 375 degrees for 45 minutes.

Tole Roberts' Meat Loaf

1-pound Bob Evans mild sausage (or any good sausage)
1-pound ground chuck
1-pound ground old fashioned ham
1 ½ cup cracker crumbs
1 cup milk
3 eggs
1 cup chopped onion
½ tsp. pepper
Salt to taste
Bread crumbs (homemade or store bought)

Mix all ingredients together. Bake in preheated 375-degree oven for 1 hour or until done.

Bread Crumbs: 3 slices lightly toasted bread, broken up. ½ tsp. seasoned salt, ½ tsp. garlic powder, and ½ tsp. paprika. Put bread and spices in blender on crumb.

Brenda's Lasagna

1-pound beef or mild Italian sausage
3 cups (28 ounce) jar spaghetti sauce *I use Prego
1 16-ounce box lasagna noodles (work according to package direction)
4 cups (2 pounds) ricotta cheese
2 cups (8 ounce) shredded mozzarella cheese
¼ cup grated parmesan cheese
4 eggs
1 tablespoon chopped parsley
1 teaspoon salt
¼ teaspoon black pepper

Brown meat, drain, and add sauce and simmer 10 minutes. Combine cheeses, eggs, parsley, salt, and pepper for filling. Pour ½ cup meat sauce in bottom of 13x9 pan. Arrange 4 pieces of lasagna noodles, cover with 1 cup meat sauce and 1/3 of cheese filling. Repeat layers of noodles, cheese and meat sauce 2 more times. Top with layer of noodles, remaining sauce and additional parmesan cheese. Bake at 350 degrees until bubbly.

Chicken Casserole

2 cups cooked chicken
1 can chicken and rice soup
½ cup chopped celery
1 small can mushroom
1 small can evaporate milk
1 can cream of mushroom soup
1 small can Chinese noodles

Mix all ingredients and bake at 350 degrees for 1 hour.

Fried Rabbit

After skinning and dressing the rabbit, cut it into pieces and wash it well. Roll the rabbit in flour and add salt and pepper to taste. Place the rabbit in hot grease in an iron skillet. Turn the heat down a little and fry into brown. It is like frying chicken.

Fried rabbit was one of my favorite meals growing up. After I married, I was hungry for fried rabbit. Mac was never a hunter; however, I asked him to get a rabbit. He said he would, but I would have to skin and dress it. I told him that wouldn't be a problem. He went hunting and not long after, he came back with the rabbit. He said he felt like a murderer. I immediately skinned and dressed the rabbit. Be sure to wash well and get the bullet out.

Glazed Country Ham

10-12-pound ham
1 cup orange juice
1 cup brown sugar
1 cup bourbon
1 tablespoon ground cloves

Place ham in a heavy-duty plastic bag. Mix remaining ingredients together and pour over ham. Close bag and refrigerate overnight.

To bake ham, remove from bag, reserving marinade. Place ham in roasting pan and bake at 325 degrees for 2 hours. Remove skin from ham, score fat in 1-inch diamonds and insert a clove in each diamond. Baste with marinade sauce and bake for 1 more hour.

Venison Steak

2 pounds venison steaks
1 cup of buttermilk
1 cup flour
Salt and pepper to taste
Lard or oil

In a medium bowl, combine the steaks and buttermilk to soak one hour in the refrigerator. Remove steaks and drain. Sprinkle steaks with salt and pepper to taste. Tenderize until ½-inch thick. Place flour in a medium bowl. Roll steaks in flour to coat. Set aside. Heat lard or oil in a large iron skillet over medium-high. Add steaks and cook until browned on both sides, approximately four minutes per side. Be sure not to overcook or the venison will become dry and tough. Serve with gravy.

Fried Frog Legs

Soak the frog legs overnight in salt water or the frog legs will jump. Also cut a slice in the legs to keep them form jumping. When ready to fry, drain, and wash again. Mix one egg, a half and half mixture of cornmeal and flour, salt, and pepper into a batter. Dip frog legs in batter and fry in oil in a heavy skillet, turning to brown evenly. Just be sure they are done, usually about 25 minutes.

I remember going frog gigging with Daddy. It was usually done in the summer months when the bullfrogs were feeding at the surface of the creek. I really did not like it so much, because it is usually done at night, and I would get scared. But sure did, and still do, like fried frog legs.

Shrimp Scampi

¼ cup butter
Dash of oil
2 tablespoon minced shallots
2 tablespoon minced garlic

Sauté all the above ingredients together and then add:
1-pound shrimp
2 tablespoons fresh parsley
2 tablespoon lemon juice
½ cup white wine

Cook 3 to 7 minutes on medium heat. Sauce can be served with shrimp.

This recipe came from Carol Johnson. Her and her husband, Don, are excellent cooks. This is easy and so good.

Teriyaki Salmon

1-pound salmon fillets (about ¼ inch thick)
1/3 cup dry white wine or orange juice
¼ cup soy sauce
½ cup packed brown sugar
1 teaspoon ginger

Remove and discard skin from salmon. Cut salmon into 4 serving pieces. Mix soy sauce, wine, brown sugar, and ginger in shallow glass bowl. Add fish and turn several times to coat. Cover and refrigerate for 1 hour, turning once. Set over to broil. Spray boiler pan rack with cooking spraying. Remove salmon from marinade and reserve the marinade. Place salmon on rack in broiler pan. Bush with marinade. Broil with top of salmon about 4 inches from heat for 5 to 6 minutes, or until salmon flakes. Discard remaining marinade.

Malvery Roberts Begley at Oneida, Clay County, Kentucky

Poppy Seed Chicken

1-1/2 pounds boneless skinless chicken
2 cans cream of chicken soup
8-ounce sour cream
1 tablespoon poppy seed
1 stick butter
Ritz crackers, about 1 sleeve

Place chicken in a pan and cover with water and bring to a boil, then reduce heat and simmer until tender and no longer pink (about 10 minutes). Once cool cut into bite size pieces. Mix together chicken soup, sour cream, chicken and poppy seed. Put into a greased 8 x12-inch or 9 x 13-inch casserole dish. Crush crackers with melted butter. Place crust topping on casserole. Bake, uncovered, at 350 degrees for about 30 minutes, or until bubbly.

This recipe came from my friend, JoAnn Ranton. It is so good!

Pop Sibley's Texas Chicken-Fried Steak

1 ½ pounds rounded steak, tenderized
1 cup flour
1 teaspoon salt
Pepper to taste
2 eggs, slightly beaten
½ cup milk
Oil for frying

Gravy:
6 tablespoons bacon or pan drippings
6 tablespoons flour
3 cups hot milk
Salt and pepper to taste

Trim steak and cut into 5 pieces. Combine flour, salt and pepper. Dredge all steak pieces in flour mixture until lightly coated. Combine eggs and milk. Dip steak into egg mixture and dredge again in flour. Heat ½ inch of oil in a heavy skillet. Place steaks in skillet and fry until golden brown on both sides.

To make gravy, remove steaks to warm oven, retaining 6 tablespoons of drippings (or use bacon drippings). Add flour. Cook and stir until flour begins to brown. Add hot milk and stir until thickened. Season with salt and pepper to taste and pour over warm steaks. Or, if you prefer, serve gravy on the side.

Mac's father, Fred, was one of the best fry cooks that I have ever met.

Mom Sibley's Meat Balls

1-pound hamburger meat
1 large potato grated
1 carrot, grated
1 onion, grated
1 egg, well beaten
Salt and pepper to taste
2 tablespoon evaporated milk

Mix all together, form into balls, brown lightly; place in baking dish and cover with one can cream of mushroom soup (diluted with equal part of water and heated). Cover and bake for one hour at 350 degrees.

Mom, Gladys Middleton Sibley, would make this dish a lot. She called it Swedish Meat Balls. Mac and I were not huge fans of the dish; however, my mother likes them and still makes them.

Roast Raccoon

1 raccoon
Sliced onions
Salt and pepper

Skin, draw, and clean raccoon. Let set overnight in salted water in refrigerator.

Drain, wash, and put in cooker and parboil for a few minutes. Drain, wash, and put in greased baking pan. Salt and pepper and place sliced onions on top. Bake, covered with foil, at 350 degrees until tender. Remove foil to brown.

Fried Chicken

1 broiler fryer chicken (2 ½ to 3 pounds)
1 cup buttermilk
1 cup all-purpose flour
Salt and Pepper to taste
Cooking oil for frying

Place chicken in a large dish. Pour buttermilk over the chicken, refrigerate one hour. Combine flour, salt and pepper in double strength paper bag. Drain chicken; toss pieces, one at a time, in flour mixture. Shake off excess flour and place on wax paper for 15 minutes. Heat oil in heavy skillet. Fry until brown on all sides. Cover and simmer, turning occasionally, for 30 minutes, or until juices run clear. Uncover and cook 5 minutes longer. Remove chicken and keep warm.

Dr. Pepper Pulled Pork Sandwiches

3-4 pounds pork loin
Pork seasonings (seasoned salt, cracked black pepper, garlic power, mustard powder or cayenne)
3 cloves garlic finely chopped
2 sweet onions thinly sliced
¼ cup barbecue sauce
12-20 ounces Dr. Pepper

For this recipe, you can season the pork loin simply, with salt and pepper, or use your favorite seasoning salt or mix of spices and herbs.

Coat a slow cooker with nonstick cooking spray or brush with oil. Season the pork loin generously (can be done the night before), coat with garlic and place it in the slow cooker. Top the pork with onion slices and barbecue sauce, then pour in enough Dr. Pepper to cover.

Cook on low heat about 8 hours or on high 4 hours. Shred the meat with two forks, allowing the mixture to soak up the sauce. Serve on buns with extra sauce, sliced onions and pickles.

Fried Mutton

The hams are used for frying. The way it is prepared at the Roberts' reunion is to remove the fat and cut the meat into 2-3-inches pieces. Season the meat with salt and pepper and then roll lightly in flour, shaking off the excess. Melt a generous amount of lard in a cast iron skillet. Place mutton in the pan and dry. Turn a few times and fry until brown.

When Mother prepares it at home, she does not use flour. She will season the meat with salt and pepper and place it in iron skillet that has a tablespoon or so of hot grease.

Cooked Mutton

Place lamb pieces in a Dutch Oven, cover with water and add salt and pepper to taste. Cook until tender. Mother likes to have sweet potatoes with her cooked mutton.

Charlie and Avis Roberts

Henry and Malvery Roberts

Breads, Rolls, & Pastries

Ola Roberts Baker, David Roberts, Malvery Roberts Begley,
Cynthia Begley Thompson, Charles Roberts, and Brenda Begley Baker.
Sitting in front Linda Roberts Sibley and Avis Begley

Homestead Cornbread

1 cup Shawnee Best White Corn Bread
2 teaspoon baking powder
¾ teaspoon salt
¾ cup milk
1 unbeaten egg
1 tablespoon melted shortening

Preheat oven to 425 degrees. Combine dry ingredients. Add milk, egg, melted shortening, and mix well. Pour into well-greased 6-inch square pan and bake at 425 degrees for 25-30 minutes.

Quick and Easy Yeast Rolls

2 packets yeast
1 ½ cups warm milk
4 tablespoon sugar
4 tablespoon oil
1 teaspoon salt
2 eggs
5 cups flour

Stir yeast and warm milk together to dissolve. Add sugar, salt, oil, and eggs and stir well. Stir in 2 cups of the flour, stirring until smooth. Cover with cloth and place on rack over hot water. Let rise 15 minutes. Stir down. Add remainder of flour, stirring until well mixed. Knead for 3 minutes. (if sticky, add ½ cup flour).

Divide into rolls. Place into 9x13-inch pan and brush tops with butter, Cover and place over hot water to rise for 25 minutes. Bake at 425 degrees for 12 minutes.

I got this recipe from cousin Margaret Roy of Ola, Yell County, Arkansas.

Aunt Quata's Angel Biscuits

1 pkg. yeast
2 tablespoon warm water
2 cups buttermilk
5 cups all-purpose flour
¼ sugar
1 tablespoon baking powder
1 tsp. baking soda
1 cup shortening
1 tsp. salt

Combine yeast and warm water. Let stand 5 minutes, or until bubbly. Add buttermilk and set aside. Combine dry ingredients. Cut in shortening. Add buttermilk mixture. Turn on floured biscuits. Bake at 400 degrees on greased baking sheet 10 to 12 minutes. Dough can be refrigerated for days.

Beer Bread

3 cups self-rising flour *Martha White's Hot-Rise flour
1 tablespoon sugar
1 beer, room temperature *Shiner Beer, if you can get it

Combine dry ingredients. Add beer and mix to make soft dough. Turn out into a greased 8x4 ½ - inch loaf pan. Set aside 15 minutes to rise. Bake at 375 degrees for 40 minutes or until brown.

This bread slices best when cold; or may be torn apart and eaten hot with butter. It's delicious toasted and served with preserves.

Anzac Biscuits

2 cups rolled oats
1 cup plain all-purpose flour
2/3 cup caster (superfine) sugar
¾ cup desiccated coconut
1/3 cup golden syrup
125 grams (about 2/3 cup) unsalted butter
1 teaspoon bicarbonate of (Baking) Soda
2 tablespoons hot water

1. Preheat oven to 160 degrees C (325 degrees). Place the oats, flour, sugar and coconut in a bowl and mix to combine.
2. Place the golden syrup and butter in a saucepan over low heat and cook, stirring, until melted. Combine the bicarbonate of soda with the water and add to the butter mixture. Pour into the oat mixture and mix well to combine.
3. Place tablespoonfuls of the mixture onto baking trays lined with non-sticking baking paper and flatten to 7 cm rounds, allowing room to spread. Bake for 8-10 minutes or until deep golden. Allow to cool on baking trays for 5 minutes before transferring to wire racks to cool.

This recipe came from cousin Melissa Juelich of Sydney, Australia. Melissa said this was a recipe from her Nanna, Evelyn Middleton. She said that the Anzac biscuits have long been associated with the Australian and New Zealand Army Corps (ANZAC) established in World War I. The biscuits were sent by wives and women's groups to soldiers abroad because the ingredients do not spoil easily, and the biscuits kept well during naval transportation.

Olivia Juelich

Buttery Cheesy Chive Muffins

2 cups self-rising flour
½ cup sour cream
2 sticks melted butter
8 oz. chive and onion cream cheese
½ cup shredded sharp cheese

Mix together ingredients well. Lightly spray a muffin pan and fill. Bake for 30 minutes at 350 degrees.

My daughter, Dr. Cynthia Sibley-Thayer, makes these muffins. So good.

Orange Date Pecan Bread

½ cup butter
¼ cup sugar
½ cup light brown sugar
2 eggs, beaten
4 teaspoons grated orange peel
½ teaspoon vanilla
½ cup sour cream
½ cup orange juice
2 ½ cups flour
1 teaspoon baking powder
1 teaspoon soda
½ teaspoon salt
1 cup chopped dates
½ cup pecans, chopped

Cream butter and sugars in large mixing bowl. Add eggs, orange peel and vanilla and beat until light and fluffy. Add sour cream and orange juice and beat thoroughly. Sift flour, baking powder, soda and salt. Add to creamed mixture and stir until blended. Fold in dates and pecans and pour into greased 9x5-inch loaf pan. Bake at 350 degrees for 60-70 minutes or until bread tests done. Allow to cool in pan for 10 minutes, remove and cool on a rack. Serve with cream cheese.

Mother's Batty Cakes

1 cup cornmeal
½ teaspoon soda
½ teaspoon salt
1 ½ cups buttermilk
1 beaten egg

Combine cornmeal, soda, and salt. Stir in buttermilk and egg. For each cake, pour 1 tablespoon batter onto hot, well-greased griddle. Fry until golden brown, turning once. Makes four servings.

Grandma Ida Begley's Cornbread

1 cup white cornmeal
1 cup flour
1 teaspoon salt
3 teaspoon baking powder
1 cup buttermilk
½ cup boiling water
1 tablespoon Crisco

Mix dry ingredients. Add buttermilk. Slowly add water to a medium consistency. Pour into a very hot iron skillet that has been on medium-high on the stove top for several minutes, melting the Crisco. Let cook for a minute or until the mixture starts to bubble. Bake at 400 degrees for 30 to 40 minutes until golden brown.

Isabelle's Cornbread

2 cup self-rising cornmeal
1 cup flour
1 egg
1 cup buttermilk

Mix all at one time. Add water to mixture, if needed. Bake in cast iron skillet at 400 degrees until brown. Isabelle Roberts Begley is a wonderful cook.

Brenda's Sour Cream Cornbread

1 ¼ cups self-rising buttermilk cornmeal mix
1 (15 ounce) can creamed corn
1 cup sour cream
¼ cup vegetable oil
3 large eggs, lightly beaten

Preheat oven to 450 degrees. Spray a well-seasoned 10-inch cast-iron skillet with nonstick cooking spray.

In a medium bowl, combine cornmeal mix, creamed corn, sour cream, oil and eggs. Pour mixture into skillet and bake for 30 minutes or until lightly browned.

*I add chopped jalapeños for taste. It is so good.

Mother's Muffins

1 ¾ cups all-purpose flour
1/3 cup sugar
2 teaspoons baking powder
¼ teaspoon salt
1 beaten egg
¾ cup milk
¼ cup cooking oil

In a mixing bowl combine flour, sugar, baking powder and ¼ teaspoon salt. Make a well in the center. Combine eggs, milk, and oil; add all at once to flour mixture. Stir just till moistened (batter should be lumpy). Lightly grease muffin cups or line with paper bake cups; fill 2/3 full. Bake in 400-degree oven about 20 minutes or until golden. Remove from pans; serve warm. Makes 10 to 12.

*Jelly Muffins: Prepare as above, except do not use paper bake cups. Fill muffin cups 1/3 full of batter, top each with 1 teaspoon jelly, Jam, or preserves, then top with enough batter to fill each muffin cup 2/3 full.

Hemmer Roberts' Hoe Cake-Corn Dodger

4 cups cornmeal
Boiling water
1 teaspoon salt
1 tablespoon bacon drippings

Pour enough boiling water over cornmeal to make dough. Add bacon drippings and salt. Shape into over pones. Bake in greased baking pans at 425 degrees until brown on both sides.

The title Hoe Cake came from workers in the fields who first cooked this bread on hoes over small campfires. Cousin Hemmer remembers cooking this bread on top of the stove in a cast iron skillet in the early 1930's.

Mother's Corn Fritters

2 cups flour
2 ½ tablespoons sugar
2 teaspoons baking powder
Pinch of salt
1 cup milk
2 eggs, beaten
1 cup corn kernels
Oil for deep-frying

Have oil heating in fryer. Sift flour, sugar, baking powder, and salt together. Add milk, eggs, and corn. Stir until combined. Drop mixture by teaspoonfuls into 375-degree oil and deep-fry, turning once until golden. Yield 6-8 servings.

Mexican Cornbread

1 ½ cup self-rising meal
2/3 cup oil
1 can cream style corn
3 eggs
1 cup buttermilk
½ cup onion
½ cup bell pepper
4 or 5 jalapeno peppers
1 cup grated cheese

Mix the self-rising meal, oil, corn, eggs, buttermilk, onion, and peppers together. Sprinkle the cheese on top. Bake at 400 degrees for 30 minutes. This recipe came from Aunt Ola Roberts Baker.

Easy Buttermilk Biscuits

2 cups all-purpose flour
1 teaspoon salt
½ teaspoon soda
2 teaspoon baking powder
4 tablespoon Crisco shortening (I use butter flavor)
1 cup buttermilk

Mix flour, soda, baking powder, and salt. Cut in Crisco, add buttermilk. Mix and then turn onto floured surface. Roll or pat our and cut into biscuits. Bake at 450 degrees for 10-15 minutes.

This recipe is in one of my old family cookbooks. It is from Linda Rash Roberts.

Cranberry Nut Bread

2 cups sifted flour
1 teaspoon baking soda
1 teaspoon salt
¾ cups sugar
1 egg
1/3 cup orange juice
1 cup chopped nuts
3 tablespoon vinegar plus water to make 2/3 cup
1 teaspoon grated orange rind
¼ cup melted shortening
1 cup halves or coarsely chopped raw cranberries

Sift together flour, soda, salt, and sugar in a mixing bowl. Beat egg, add liquids, orange rind and melted shortening. Add all at once to flour mixture, stirring until flour is just dampened. Add cranberries and nuts and stir just enough to blend well. Turn into a greased loaf pan. Bake in a moderate 350-degree oven, 60-70 minutes or until done. Remove from the pan and cool thoroughly on a rack. Slice or wrap in foil or Saran Wrap to keep fresh and moist, and this type of tea bread gets better every day.

This is recipe came from Effie Samuels. One of the great cooks of Sardis United Methodist Church. This bread is so good.

Mandarin Orange and Cranberry Muffin Bread

2 cups self-rising flour
½ cup sugar
1 egg, beaten
1 ¼ cup milk
2 tablespoons butter
½ teaspoon vanilla extract
1 cup fresh whole cranberries
11 ounce can mandarin orange, drained

Whisk together the flour and sugar. Add in the melted butter, egg, milk and vanilla extract. Stir well to combine, then fold in the cranberries and mandarin oranges. Butter a loaf pan very well and pour the mixture into the pan and spread around to even out. Bake at 375 degrees for 35 to 40 minutes or until a toothpick comes out clean. Remove from the pan to cooling rack.

Banana Nut Bread

½ cup shortening
1 ½ cup sugar
2 cups flour
½ teaspoon salt
½ cup chopped pecans
½ teaspoon baking powder
2 eggs, unbeaten
4 tablespoon milk
2 large bananas mashed

Cream shortening and sugar. Sift dry ingredients and add to creamed mixture. Add 1 egg at a time and mix well. Add milk, bananas and nuts. Bake in a greased loaf pan at 350 degree for 1 hour or more.

Apple Cake Bread

2 cups finely chopped peeled apple
1 cup sugar
1 teaspoon cinnamon
Set aside for 30 minutes

Mix together the following:
1 egg beaten
½ cup vegetable oil
1 ½ cup flour
¼ teaspoon salt
1 teaspoon soda
1 cup chopped pecans

Mix well and add apple mixture. Bake in greased, floured loaf pan for 1 hour at 350 degrees. This is a very moist bread and wonderful for the holiday season.

Recipe came from cousin, Sonia Bullard Caldwell, of Apache, Oklahoma. I made it my recipe.

Boone Tavern Spoon Bread

1 ¼ cup white cornmeal
1 ½ cu teaspoons baking powder
1 teaspoon salt
2 tablespoons butter
3 cups milk
3 eggs

Stir cornmeal into rapidly boiling milk. Cook until very thick, stirring constantly, to prevent boiling over. Remove from fire and allow to cool. The mixture will be cold and very stiff. Add well beaten eggs, salt, baking powder, and melted butter. Beat with mixer 15 minutes. Pour into well-greased casserole. Bake 30 minutes at 375 degrees.

Boone Tavern Corn Sticks

½ cup flour
2 cups white cornmeal
½ teaspoon salt
1 teaspoon baking powder
½ teaspoon soda
2 cups buttermilk
2 eggs, well beaten
¼ cup melted lard

Sift flour, cornmeal, salt, and baking powder into bowl. Add mixture of soda and buttermilk; mix well. Add eggs and lard, mixing well after each addition. Place greased corn stick plan in 450-500-degree oven until pan smokes. Pour batter into prepared pan. Bake at 450 degrees for 18 minutes or until golden brown. *It is important to heat the greased pan before filling with batter to get the corn sticks crisp outside. Yields 12 corn sticks.

Zucchini Bread

3 eggs
1 cup vegetable oil
2 cups sugar
2 cups grated zucchini
2 cups flour
¼ teaspoon baking powder
½ teaspoon salt
2 teaspoon cinnamon
2 teaspoon soda
2 teaspoon vanilla
1 ½ cups chopped nuts

Beat eggs, oil, and sugar well. Add flour, soda, baking powder, salt, cinnamon, and vanilla. Mix well, add nuts and zucchini and mix. Spray or grease pans. Makes 2 loaves. Bake at 350 degrees for approximately 45 minutes.

Fred Mac Sibley picking Black Walnuts on the Kentucky farm

Cornbread Dressing

1 large pan baked cornbread cooled
Toasted light bread or biscuits
1 large chopped onion
1 cup butter
Pepper and Salt to taste
Sage to taste
Poultry seasoning to taste
1-2 boxes of chicken broth
Fresh washed and chopped celery to taste

We have never had a written recipe for cornbread dressing until now. Sauté onions and celery in the chicken broth. Add one cup of butter. Let it cook until the onions and celery become soft. With hands, crumble cornbread and light bread together. I like to use just toasted, plain white sandwich loaf bread. Add salt, pepper, sage, and poultry seasoning. Stir in the broth with onions and celery. Taste and be sure it has the seasoning amounts that you like. Add more seasoning if needed. I like my mixture a little soupy. If it is dry, add more chicken stock. Also, if possible, add some of the drippings of the chicken or turkey to the mixture. Turn mixture into large roasting pan. I like to add a little more butter on the top. Bake in preheated 350 degrees oven for about 30 minutes or so until top of dressing is hot and a little brown on top.

Granny would have added eggs to her cornbread, probably three. Also, she would have used left over biscuits as she did not have store bought light bread. Now I throw in a package of Stovetop Dressing just to bring up the flavors.

Mother's Chocolate Cream Pie

Mix in saucepan:
1 ½ cups sugar
½ cup cocoa
3 tablespoon cornstarch
½ teaspoon salt
3 cups milk

Cook, stirring constantly, until mixture thickens and boils. Boil 1 minute. Remove from heat. Gradually stir in half of the hot mixture into 3 slightly beaten egg yolks. Then blend into hot mixture in sauce pan. Boil 1 minute more, stirring constantly. Blend in 1 tablespoon butter, 1 ½ teaspoon vanilla. Cool just a little.

Pour into baked 9-inch pie shell. Cover with meringue. Bake at 400 degrees until meringue is lightly brown.

This is my favorite pie. All through the years when I would come home for a visit, I knew my mother would make me her Chocolate Cream Pie.

Indiana Cream Pie

Mix:
1 cup half & half
1 ½ cup milk
1 cup brown sugar
¼ cup cornstarch
¼ cup butter
1 tsp. vanilla (add last)

Cook until thickened, add vanilla and beat thoroughly. Pour into baked pie shell and bake at 325 degrees for 20 minutes. Put a little nutmeg on top.

Mac and I went to Bluffton, Indiana to visit friends. While there the United Methodist Women's group had a dinner for us. This pie was made by a lady in her late 80's. I told my friend that I wanted the recipe and she told me this lady had always flatly refused to give her recipe to anyone. I went up anyway and started talking to her about being president of a United Methodist Women's District in Texas. She gave me the recipe, if I promised not to give it to my Indiana friends.

Texas Pecan Pie

3 eggs
1 cup pecans
3 tablespoon flour
1 cup white syrup
3 tablespoon butter
1 tablespoon vanilla
1 cup sugar
1 unbaked pie shell

Beat eggs; add sugar, flour, syrup, butter and vanilla; mix well. Stir in pecans. Pour into shell and bake at 350 degrees for about 1 hour.

This is the pie I make most often. It is between this recipe and the one from Smith County, Texas. Both are good.

Jefferson Davis Pie

1 unbaked pie shell
2 cups brown sugar
1 tablespoon flour
½ tsp. nutmeg
1 cup heavy cream
4 eggs, slightly beaten
1 cup heavy cream
1 tsp. lemon juice
½ tsp. lemon zest
½ cup melted butter

In a large mixing bowl, combine sugar, flour, and nutmeg and mix well. Add cream and mix. Add eggs and mix. Add lemon juice, lemon zest and melted butter and mix well. Pour mixture into pie shell and bake at 375 degrees for 45 minutes. Cool and serve with whipped cream.

This recipe is one used at the Boone Tavern in Berea, Kentucky. Boone Tavern is famous for preparing traditional foods in Kentucky. This pie was a favorite of Jefferson Davis, president of the Confederate States of America, who was born in Kentucky. Papa Roberts always said we were kin to Jefferson Davis.

Sweet Potato Pie

1 cup sweet potatoes
3 ½ cup sugar
1 rounded teaspoon nutmeg
6 eggs
1 stick butter melted
1 cup milk
2 (9-inch) pie shells

Cream together sweet potatoes, sugar, and nutmeg. Add eggs, one at a time. Pour in melted butter and blend. Mix in the milk. Pour this mixture into 2 unbaked pie shells and bake for 1 hour or longer at 350 degrees until brown.

Pecan Pie (Smith County, Texas)

4 eggs
1 cup sugar
4 tablespoon flour
1 stick butter melted and cooled
2 cups (16 oz.) white corn syrup
Pinch salt
4 teaspoons vanilla
1 teaspoon almond extract
2-1/2 to 3 cups pecans
2 pie shells, uncooked

Beat eggs; add sugar and flour. Add butter, corn syrup, salt, vanilla, and almond extract; mix well. Stir in pecans and fill 2 uncooked pie shells. Bake in preheated oven at 350 degrees, about 1 hour.

Dried Apple Fried Pies

Dough:
2 ½ cups self-rising flour
2 tablespoons granulated sugar
½ cup shortening
¾ cup buttermilk

Apple Filling:
1 (5 ounces) package died apples
2 tablespoons granulated sugar
2 tablespoons light brown sugar
1 ½ teaspoon fresh lemon juice
¼ teaspoon ground cinnamon
1/8 teaspoon table salt

Cinnamon Sugar:
¼ cup granulated sugar
1 tablespoon ground cinnamon

Remaining Ingredient: Vegetable oil

1. Prepare dough: Stir together flour and sugar. Cut shortening into flour mixture with a pastry blend or fork until crumbly. Add buttermilk, stirring just until dry ingredients are moistened. Shape dough into a disk; wrap in plastic wrap. Chill 12 to 24 hours.

2. Meanwhile, prepare filling: Bring apples and water to cover (about 3 ½ cups) to a boil in a large saucepan over medium-high heat. Reduce heat to low, and simmer, stirring occasionally, 1 hour. Remove from heat; cover and let stand 1 hour.

3. Drain apples; place in a large bowl. Coarsely mash apples with 2 tablespoons granulated sugar and next 4 ingredients. (A pastry blender does a great job.) Cover and chill 12 hours to 24 hours.

4. Prepare cinnamon sugar: Stir together 1/4cup granulated sugar and 1 tablespoon Cinnamon. *Double.

5. Pour oil to depth of 2 inches into a Dutch oven; heat over medium-high heat to 350 degrees. Turn dough out onto a lightly floured surface. Divide into 16 portions; shape into balls. Flatten into 3-inch circles; roll into 5-inch circles. Working with 1 circle at a time, spoon 1 tablespoon filling into center of each circle; brush edge with water. Fold dough over filling. Use the tones of a fork to seal.

6. Fry, in batches, in hot oil 3 to 4 minutes or until golden. When frying they should float when they are done. Transfer to a paper towel-lined baking sheet. Sprinkle both sides of hot pies with cinnamon sugar.

Brenda's Dried Apple Fried Pies

Golden Lamb Shaker Sugar Pie

½ cup soft butter
¼ cup flour
1 cup brown sugar
2 cups Half & Half
½ teaspoon vanilla
Nutmeg
1-9-inch unbaked pie crust

Preheat oven to 350 degrees. Mix flour and sugar and place in bottom of pie shell. Combine butter, Half & Half and vanilla. Pour into pie shell. Sprinkle nutmeg on top. Bake 40-50 minutes or until firm.

Five Minute Key Lime Pie

¼ cup water
1 package (4-serving size) lime flavor gelatin
2 containers (6 oz.) Key Lime Pie yogurt
1-8 oz. Cool Whip
1-Graham Pie Crust
Directions:
In microwave safe measuring cup heat water on high to 45 seconds to 1-1/2 minutes or boiling. Whisk in gelatin until dissolved.
In large bowl whisk together, gelatin mixture and yogurt. Fold in whipped topping. Carefully spread in crust. Refrigerate at least 4 hours or until set. Garnish as desired. Store in refrigerator.

Cleo's Pineapple Pie

1 stick butter
1-1/2 cup sugar
1-1/2 tablespoon flour
½ tsp. vanilla
3 eggs
1 small can crush pineapple (do not drain)

Mix in that order with spoon. Pour in unbaked 9-inch pie shell. Bake 30 to 45 minutes at 350 degrees. This pie is so easy and good. Recipe came from aunt Cleo Roberts Massner.

10 Minute German Chocolate Pie

4-ounce German Sweet Chocolate bar
1/3 cup milk
2 tablespoons sugar
3-ounce cream cheese softened
8-ounce Cool Whip thawed
1 prepared graham crackers pie crust

Melt chocolate with 2 tablespoons of milk in the microwave or low heat, stirring until chocolate is melted and smooth. Beat sugar into cream cheese. Add remaining milk and chocolate mixture. Beat until smooth. Fold in Cool Whip. Spoon into crust, and chill until firm, usually overnight. I like to add chocolate curls before serving the pie. I have made this a lot for church events.

Lemon Pie

Mix ¾ cup of sugar
3 tablespoon flour
1-1/2 tablespoons melted butter
1/3 cup lemon juice
½ cup milk
2 egg yolks

Mix well. Bake 350 degrees in uncooked crust for 30 minutes.
Meringue – 2 egg whites and 1/3 cup sugar. Mix. Place on cooled pie and put under boiler until brown.

*When I make this filling, I sometimes double the recipe. The original recipe just does not seem enough to fill a 9-inch pie shell.

Jennie is Mac's grandmother. He can remember his mother, Gladys, making this pie and always saying it was her mother's recipe.

Jennie Atlantic Gray Middleton

Transparent Pie

Melt two sticks of Oleo (butter). Add 2 cups sugar and beat. Add 4 eggs, one at a time, and beat together. Add 2 teaspoon lemon juice, 1 teaspoon vanilla, and 2 tablespoons white Karo syrup. Put into tart shells or pie shell and bake 10 minutes at 450 degrees, then 10 more minutes at 350 degrees.

Cousin, David Dino Roberts, remembers his mother, Patricia Ann Sauer Roberts, making this pie when he was growing up.

Banana Pudding

½ cup sugar
2 tablespoon flour
¼ teaspoon salt
2 cups milk
2 eggs
1 teaspoon vanilla
Vanilla wafers
4 large bananas

Combine sugar, flour, and salt in double boiler; stir in milk. Cook over boiling water, stirring, until thickened. Cook for 15 minutes longer, stirring occasionally, Cool. Beat eggs, stir into cooled mixture gradually. Cook for 5 minutes, stirring constantly. Remove from heat; add vanilla.

Line bowl with wafers; top with sliced bananas. Pour part of the custard over bananas. Continue layers, ending with wafers on top. Serve warm or chilled.
Yield 6 servings.

Mother would make a meringue and place on top.

Ulysses Creek Blackberry Cobbler

1 cup sugar
1 cup self-rising flour
1-quart blackberries
1 cup milk

Mix sugar, flour and milk together. Pour into an iron skillet. Place blackberries over mixture. Cut one stick of butter over berries. Sprinkle sugar over berries. Bake in 350 degrees oven for one hour.

This recipe is one that Uncle Charles E. Roberts remembers his mother making for him. It has always been a favorite.

Butterscotch Pie

6 tablespoon butter
1 cup dark brown sugar
2/3 cup boiling water
3 tablespoons cornstarch
½ tsp. salt
2 tablespoons flour
2 cups milk
3 eggs separated
1 tsp. vanilla
3 tablespoon sugar

Melt butter in heavy skillet over lot heat. Add brown sugar and cook until foamy, stirring constantly. Add boiling water. Remove from heat. Mix cornstarch, flour, and salt in the top of a double boiler. Stir in milk and brown sugar syrup. Cook until it thickens, stirring constantly. Remove from heat and stir a little of mixture into beaten egg yolks then blend into the hot mixture. Cook over hot water about 5 minutes. Add vanilla. Pour into baked 9-inch pie shell.

Beat egg whites, adding 1 tablespoon sugar at a time. Beat until stiff. Spread on pie and bake at 350 degrees until light brown.

Florence Begley Cochran gave me this recipe a long time ago. It was one that her mother, Nancy Margaret Wooton Begley made when she was growing up in Bowlingtown, Perry County, Kentucky.

Brenda's Apple Pie

5-7 tart apples (5-6 cups)
1 cup sugar
2 tablespoons flour
Dash salt
1 teaspoon cinnamon
¼ teaspoon nutmeg
2 tablespoons butter

Line 9-inch pie plate with bottom crust.

Peel apples, slicing thinly. Toss in ½ teaspoon lemon juice. In a bowl mix sugar, salt, and spices. Toss apples in mixture. Fill pastry lined pie pan. Top with butter slices and then top crust. Cut slits in crust. Bake in 375 degrees oven for 1 hour or until it bubbles out of top slits in crust.

Sour Cherry Pie

2 (16 ounces) cans pitted tart red cherries
1 ½ cups sugar, divided
1/3 cup corn starch
1 tablespoon butter or margarine
¼ teaspoon almond extract
3 to 4 drops red food coloring

Drain cherries and reserve 1 cup liquid. Combine ¾ cup sugar, 1/3 cup cornstarch and dash of salt in saucepan. Stir in 1 cup liquid. Cook and stir until thick and bubbly. Cook and stir 1 minute more. Remove from heat stir in remaining ¾ cup sugar, drained cherries, almond extract, and butter. Add 3 to 4 drops red food coloring and stir gently. Pour into prepared pastry. Bake 400 degrees for 10 minutes. Reduce to 350 degrees for 45 minutes.

Brenda and her granddaughter, Hannah, making Sour Cherry Pie

Kentucky Bread Pudding with Bourbon Sauce

6 cold biscuits or 8 to 10 slices cold bread crumbled
1 cup hot water
1 cup sugar
¼ cup butter melted
1 teaspoon vanilla flavoring
1 teaspoon nutmeg
1 cup raisins soaked in ¼ cup Kentucky Bourbon whiskey. If you leave out the raisins, just soak nuts in the bourbon
2 eggs beaten
½ cup evaporated milk
1 cup pecans or walnuts

Place biscuits or bread in greased or sprayed baking dish. Pour hot water over biscuits or bread and let soak about 10 minutes. Mix remaining ingredients together and pour over bread. Sprinkle nuts and raisins on top. Bake at 350 degrees for 30 to 40 minutes until brown. Makes about 8 servings.

Bourbon Sauce:

1 cup sugar
6 tablespoon melted butter
½ cup buttermilk
1 tablespoon bourbon or whatever amount is good for you. *I use Woodford Reserve made in Kentucky
½ teaspoon baking soda
1 tablespoon white corn syrup
1 teaspoon vanilla

Combine all ingredients and boil for 1 minutes. Either pour the sauce over the pudding and let soak in or serve separately so each person can add their own. Or you can pour about half over the pudding and save the other half for sauce.
Pudding can be served hot or cold. Sauce will keep in refrigerator for several days.

Cakes, Cookies, & Desserts

Malvery Roberts Begley & Isabelle Roberts Begley

Kentucky Pecan Bourbon Cake

3 cups sifted flour
2 teaspoon baking powder
2 teaspoon nutmeg
2 cups sugar
1 cup butter (2 sticks)
6 eggs separated
1-pound pecans coarsely chopped
1-pound golden raisins
1 jar (4 ounces) or more diced candied fruit, finely chopped
1 cup Bourbon Whiskey

Grease the bottom and sides of a 10-inch Angel Food cake pan; line entire surface with brown paper; grease paper.

Mix 2 tablespoons of the flour with the pecans and candied fruit; reserve. Stir the remaining flour with the baking powder and nutmeg. Cream butter and sugar; thoroughly beat in one egg yolk at time. Beat in sifted dry ingredients alternately, with the bourbon; if necessary, continue to beat until batter is very smooth.

Stir in pecans and fruit mixture. Beat egg whites until stiff; fold into batter so there are no blobs of white left. Turn into the prepared pan. Bake in a very slow (250 degrees) oven for four hours, or until cake tester inserted in center comes out clean. Place a shallow pan of water on top shelf of oven during the first 2-1/2 hours of baking. Place cake on wire rack to cool. Remove brown paper. Cool completely.

To store cake, dip a double piece of cheesecloth in bourbon and wrap cake in it; wrap again in transparent plastic wrapping and store in airtight metal container.

I got this recipe from Aunt Mae Bowling Roberts probably in the 1980's. Aunt Mae said she had the recipe for 40 or 45 years and she got it from the "Courier Journal".

Memaw's Blackberry Wine Cake

1 box yellow cake mix
1 small box Blackberry Jell-O *if you cannot find it; use Black Cherry
4 eggs beaten slightly
1 cup cooking oil
1 cup blackberry wine
Mix all together and pour into a greased Bundt pan. Preheat oven to 350 degrees and bake for 40 or 50 minutes.

This recipe came from a friend, Larry G. Glover, from Winnsboro, Texas

Lemon Poppy Seed Bundt Cake

Cake: 1 box lemon cake mix
1 small box instant lemon pudding
¼ cup poppy seeds
½ cup oil
1 cup water
4 eggs
Frosting: ½ cup butter, softened
1-pound powdered sugar
5 tablespoons fresh squeezed lemon juice (2-3 lemons)
Lemon zest

For cake: Preheat oven to 350 degrees. Grease and flour Bundt pan.
Mix all cake ingredients on low to medium speed until well combined.
Pour cake batter into pan; bake about 45-50 minutes. Cool completely. Remove cake from pan after cooling 10 minutes.

For frosting: Mix butter and powdered sugar on medium speed until well blended. Gradually mix in lemon juice by the tablespoon until you reach desired consistency. Stir in lemon zest.

I cannot remember where I got this recipe. But I really like it. I make it a lot.

Eva Jennings's Blackberry Cake

2/3 cup Crisco
2 cups sugar
2 eggs
3 cups flour
1 teaspoon soda
1 teaspoon cloves
1 teaspoon cinnamon
Pinch of salt
1 cup blackberry juice
2 cups raisins
1 cup nuts
2 cups blackberries

Cream shortening, sugar, and eggs. Add sifted dry ingredients with juice. Mix in berries and nuts. Bake at 350 degrees until done. Makes 3 regular cakes.

Caramel Icing:

1 stick butter
1 pound brown sugar
½ cup evaporated milk

Cook 4 minutes. After it starts to boil, remove from heat and beat until thick.

Malvery Roberts Begley & her daughters (Cynthia, Brenda and Avis)

Red Velvet Cake

2 cups flour
1 teaspoon salt
2 tablespoon cocoa
1-1/2 cup sugar
½ cup Crisco
2 (1 oz.) bottles red food coloring
2 eggs
1 teaspoon vanilla
1 cup buttermilk
1 tsp. soda
1 tablespoon vinegar

Sift flour, salt, and cocoa. In a large bowl, cream sugar and Crisco until fluffy. Add food color and eggs; beat well. Add vanilla and dry ingredients alternately with buttermilk, beating well after each addition. Mix soda and vinegar in small bowl. Fold until batter. Bake 20 minutes at 350 degrees. Use 3 (8 inch) greased and dusted cake pans. Cool and then frost.

Frosting:

1 cup milk
1/3 cup flour
¼ cup Crisco
1 stick butter
1 cup sugar
1 teaspoon vanilla
Pinch of salt

Cook milk and flour until thick. Cool. Beat Crisco, butter, sugar, vanilla, and salt in bowl. Add to flour mixture. Beat until smooth.

Aunt Quata's Buttermilk Pound Cake

3 cups sugar
1 cup Crisco
3 cups flour
1 cup buttermilk
6 eggs
¼ teaspoon soda dissolved in milk
1 teaspoon vanilla or lemon extract
¼ teaspoon salt

Cream sugar and Crisco. Add eggs one at a time. Add flour, extract, and salt. Add buttermilk and soda. Mix all together and bake in tube pan for 1 ½ hours in 350-degree oven.

Brenda's Apple Crisp

¾ cup sugar
2 tablespoon flour
¼ teaspoon salt
1 teaspoon cinnamon
2 ½ quarts apples, sliced
Mix sugar, flour, salt, and cinnamon. Add to apples and mix. Put on bottom of a greased pan.

Top Part:
1 cup oatmeal
1 cup brown sugar
1 cup flour
¼ teaspoon soda
1/3 teaspoon baking powder
2/3 cup butter

Mix ingredients till crumbly, then put on top of apples and pat firmly into 9x13 inch pan. Bake at 350 degrees for 50 minutes or until brown and crust is formed. Serve with milk or cream.

Lou Gibson's Blackberry Cake

2 sticks butter
2 cups sugar
2 cups berries, juice and all
3 cups flour
1 teaspoon cocoa
3 eggs
½ teaspoon salt
1 teaspoon cinnamon
1 teaspoon all spice
2 teaspoons soda
1 cup raisins
1 cup nuts

Prepare mixture by creaming sugar and butter; add eggs. Mix dry ingredients, add berries and juice alternating with dry ingredients. Beat until smooth. Add raisins and nuts which have been sprinkled with flour. Pour into greased floured pan and bake at 350 degrees for 1-1/2 hours or until done. Use a ten-cup bunt cake pan or a large angel food cake pan.

Frosting:

3 tablespoon butter
6 tablespoon brown sugar
9 tablespoon milk
Bring butter, brown sugar, and milk to boil. Remove from heat and stir in powdered sugar until of spreading constituency.

Pecan Brownies

1 box Butter Pecan Cake Mix
1 stick butter
1 egg

Mix together and pat in a 11x13 pan. Set aside. *I use a jelly roll pan.

1 box powdered sugar
1 8-ounce cream cheese melted
1 stick butter softened
2 eggs

Mix all together. Pour on cake mix and sprinkle with pecans. Bake 55 minutes at 300 degrees.

This is one of my go to recipes for church and social events. Easy and makes a lot.

Oatmeal Cake

1-1/2 cup boiling water
1 cup oats
½ cup Wesson oil
1 cup white sugar
1 cup brown sugar
2 eggs
1-1/2 cup flour
1 teaspoon soda
1 teaspoon cinnamon
½ teaspoon salt

Pour boiling water over oats and let cool. Beat oil and sugar together. Add eggs; beat well. Add oats. Add flour, soda, cinnamon and salt that have been sifted together. Bake 35 to 40 minutes in a 9x13-inch pan that has been greased and floured. Bake at 350 degrees.

Icing:
1 cup brown sugar
½ cup sweet milk
1 stick butter
1 can coconut
1 cup nuts
Combine sugar, butter and milk. Cook 5 minutes, then add coconut and nuts.

Mother made this cake a lot while I was growing up. I remember making it for the family.

Solera Cream Sherry Cake

1 box yellow Cake Mix
1 cup Sherry
¾ cup of oil
1 small package instant French Vanilla Pudding

Mix all ingredients in large bowl, mix for 5 minutes on medium speed. Use a lightly greased Bundt pan for cake. Bake at 350 degrees for 50 minutes.

Recipe from sister, Velma Sizemore Julian.

Fred Mac Sibley & grandson, Korbin Thayer

Texas Sheet Cake

1 cup butter
1 cup water
4 heaping teaspoon cocoa
2 cups sifted flour
2 eggs
2 cups sugar
½ teaspoon salt
½ cup sour cream
1 teaspoon soda

Combine butter, water, and cocoa in heavy saucepan. Heat to boiling, stirring. Remove from heat and add flour, sugar, and salt. Beat until well mixed. Add sour cream, soda, and eggs and mix well. Pour into greased 15x11x1-1/2- inch pan. Bake at 375 degrees for 22 minutes. Pour frosting on cake when it comes out of oven. Do not let cool.

Frosting:
½ cup butter
6 tablespoons milk
4 teaspoons cocoa
1-pound powdered sugar
1 teaspoon vanilla
1 cup chopped pecans
Combine butter, milk, and cocoa in saucepan. Heat to boiling until it bubbles. Take from heat and mix with powdered sugar, nuts, and vanilla. Frost cake.

I have made this cake hundreds of times.

Daisy's Blackberry Cake

1 cup blackberry jam
1 cup Miracle Whip salad dressing
1 cup sugar
1 cup hot water
2 tablespoons cocoa
1 tablespoons cinnamon
½ tablespoon ground allspice
3 cups flour
1-1/2 teaspoon soda
Pinch of salt
Mix gently. Bake at 300 degrees until done in center.

Icing:

1-1/2 cups brown sugar packed
¼ cup plus 2 Tbsp. milk
¼ cup plus 2 Tbsp. Crisco
Pinch of salt
¾ teaspoon vanilla

Boil Sugar, milk, Crisco, and salt, stirring constantly, 2 minutes, after it boils hard. Remove from heat and add vanilla. Beat until creamy and thick to spread. Add cream if it thickens.

This recipe came from Cleo Roberts Massner. I believe Daisy was an aunt to her husband, Earl Massner.

Better Than (Sex) Cake

1 box of yellow cake mix
2 medium bananas
1 8 ounces can crushed pineapple
1 cup sugar
1 12-ounce tub of Cool Whip
1 package of instant vanilla pudding mix
1 8-ounce package of cream cheese
Chopped pecans, optional

Bake cake according to directions. Mix pineapple and sugar together in saucepan, bring to a boil. Puncture holes in cake and pour mixture over hot cake. Let cool. Mix pudding and cream cheese together until smooth. Pour over pineapple. Slice bananas over pudding mix. Top with Cool Whip. Sprinkle with pecans.

When Mac retired from Dallas Police Department the ladies in his office made this cake, as it was his favorite.

Fresh Rhubarb Cake

½ cup (1 stick) butter
1-1/2 cup brown sugar
1 tsp. vanilla
1 egg
1 cup buttermilk
2 cups plain flour
1 teaspoon baking powder
1 teaspoon baking soda
¼ teaspoon salt
1-1/2 cups rhubarb (cut into 1-inch pieces

In mixing bowl, cream together butter, brown sugar and vanilla until well mixed. Add unbeaten eggs and buttermilk, beating well. Sift together the flour, baking powder, soda and salt. Add to mixture, beating until smooth. Stir in rhubarb. Turn into a greased and floured 9 x 13 x 2-inch cake pan.

Frosting:
Mix together 1/3 cup granulated sugar, 2 teaspoons cinnamon and ½ cup nuts. Sprinkle over top of cake. Bake at 325 – 350 degrees for 35 to 40 minutes.

This recipe came from Isabelle Roberts Begley of Avawan, Kentucky

Coconut Cream Layer Cake

2 cups granulated sugar
12 ounce sweetened shredded coconut
1 8-ounce container sour cream
1 (15.25 ounce) butter golden cake mix
1 8-ounce container frozen whipped topping thawed

1. Prepare the coconut cream filling. Stir together sugar, shredded coconut and sour cream in a bowl; cover and chill for 2 hours.
2. Line the bottom of 2 (8-inch) round cake pans with parchment paper and spray sides and bottom with vegetable cooking spray. Prepare the cake mix according to package directions. Divide batter evenly between the 2 cake pans; bake as directed. Let cool completely.
3. Cut each cake layer in half horizontally using a serrated knife, making 4 even layers. Place 1-layer cut side up, on a platter. Stir chilled coconut filling; remove and reserve 1 cup for icing. Spread about a 1 cup of the remaining coconut filling evenly over top, leaving a ½-inch border. Top with another cake layer; repeat layers twice, beginning with coconut filling and ending with a cake layer.
4. Stir together whipped topping and reserved 1 cup coconut cream filling. Spread mixture on top and sides of cake. Chill cake for at least 24 hours or up to 2 days.
Serves 12. *You can use a devil's food cake and make a Chocolate Coconut Cake.

Cleo Roberts Massner & Eugene Smallwood
& Linda Roberts Sibley

Mother's Bull Nelson Rum Cake

1 cup nuts (half pecans and half walnuts) chopped and toasted
1 pkg. yellow cake mix
1 3-ounce instant vanilla pudding
½ cup cold water
½ cup rum
4 eggs
½ cup Wesson oil

Sprinkle the nuts on the bottom of a greased tube pan. Beat the cake mix with dry pudding mix, water, oil, and rum. Beat in one egg at a time. Pour batter into pan and bake one hour at 325 degrees. Cool for 10 minutes on a wire rack and unmold. Cover hot cake with glaze.

To make glaze: Combine ¼ cup melted butter, ½ cup sugar and ¼ cup rum. Simmer five minutes. Brush on cake. Repeat once or twice as cake cools.

Mother said this cake is a combination of a rum cake from the Three Rivers Cookbook, Pittsburgh, PA. and one that she found in a newspaper. She toasts the nuts in a skillet on top of stove. All pecans may be used.

Blackberry Dumplings

1-quart blackberries (use fresh, frozen, or canned blackberries)
1 cup water
1 cup sugar
2 tablespoon butter

Put into a heavy pot, bring to boil over medium heat, then reduce heat to a simmer.

Dumplings:

2 cups all-purpose flour
½ teaspoon baking powder
½ teaspoon salt
2 tablespoon butter
½ cup milk plus more if needed to make stiff dough

Combine flour, baking powder, and salt. Cut in butter and add milk to make a stiff dough.

Roll out dough on a floured surface to about 1/8-inch thickness. Cut dough into 1 to 1 ½ inch squares. Sprinkle lightly with flour and drop into boiling berries. Cover tightly and boil gently for 10-15 minutes.

My mother also liked to use Pillsbury biscuits. Gently roll biscuits our on floured surface to about 1/8-inch thickness and cut into fourths. Drop biscuits into boiling berries. Cover tightly and boil gently for 10-15 minutes.

*Put dumplings in berries one piece at a time. Use judgment with how many dumplings to put in. Don't want so many they stick together.

This recipe came from Aunt Vinia Doyle Roberts. She wrote: "One on my favorite desserts that my mother, Mary Roark Doyle Wilson, would make is blackberry dumplings. A recipe that she learned from her mother, Sarah Hensley Craft Roark. After blackberry picking, she would can the blackberries to make blackberry dumplings or cobbler."

Apple Nut Cake

2 cups sugar
1 teaspoon soda
1 tablespoon vanilla
1 cup chopped black walnuts
1 ½ cups cooking oil
3 cups plain flour
1 teaspoon salt
3 cups peeled diced apples
1 cup coconut

Mix sugar, oil, and eggs. Beat well. Mix flour, soda, and salt. Add to first mixture along with vanilla. Mix apples, walnuts, and coconut. Add to other ingredients. Pour in to greased and floured pan. Bake 1 hour and 10 minutes at 350 degrees.

Frosting:
¼ cup butter
½ teaspoon soda
1 tablespoon white corn syrup
1 cup sugar
½ teaspoon vanilla
½ cup buttermilk

Place the ingredients in a saucepan. Stir over low heat until all is dissolved, or if you want it thicker cook 5 to 6 minutes. I like it thin.

This is an old recipe used by Thelma Slusher Sizemore.

Elmer Sizemore & Thelma Slusher Sizemore

Jewish Apple Cake

3 cups un-sifted flour
2 ½ cup sugar
1 cup cooking oil
4 eggs
½ teaspoon salt
Juice of one orange
2 ½ teaspoons vanilla
3 teaspoons baking powder

4 large apples sliced thin-add 2 teaspoons cinnamon and 5 tablespoons sugar, mix.
Grease and flour a tube pan. Preheat oven 350 degrees.
Mix flour, sugar, oil, eggs, salt, orange juice, baking powder, and vanilla until smooth. Put layer of batter in pan, add layer of apple mix, layer of batter, layer of apple mix and continue until ending with apples. Bake at 350 degrees for 1 hour and 45 minutes.

This is one of my favorite cakes to make. Been making it close to 40 years.

Ola Roberts Baker England

Linda Kekauoha's Hot Milk Cake

4 eggs
2 cups sugar
2 cups flour
Pinch of salt
3 teaspoons baking powder
2 teaspoons vanilla
1 cup milk
½ or ¼ pound of butter or margarine

Combine milk and butter in saucepan, heat until milk almost boils, be careful not to scorch milk.

Beat eggs and sugar until well blended, then add other ingredients and finally milk mixture.

Grease and flour pans.

Makes 1 tube pan, bake at 350 for about 1 hour or until top is golden.
Makes 2 layers, bake at 350 degrees for about 30-35 minutes.
Makes about 30 cupcakes, bake at 425 degrees for 15 minutes.

We prepare the batter as above leaving out the vanilla flavor. We split the batter in two separate bowls and put coconut flavor in one and orange flavor in the other, along with some orange zest.

For Vanilla Frosting:
½ cup Crisco (shortening)
1 ½ teaspoon vanilla
pinch of salt
1-pound confectioners' sugar (10x)
¼ cup of milk (more or less) to get to the consistency for spreading

For the orange frosting: I substitute orange juice for the milk and add orange zest. I have also used orange extract instead of vanilla for orange frosting.

Brown Sugar Black Walnut Cake

1 cup shortening
1 stick butter
1-pound brown sugar
5 eggs
3 cups sifted plain flour
1 teaspoon baking powder
½ teaspoon salt
1 cup evaporated milk
½ teaspoon maple flavoring
1 cup black walnuts chopped into medium pieces

Preheat the oven to 350 degrees. Cream the shortening, butter, and brown sugar together. Add the eggs, one at a time, beating well. Sift the flour with the baking powder and salt. Alternate adding the dry ingredients and the milk to the sugar mixture. Add the flavorings and mix well. Bake in a greased and floured tube pan for 1 hour and 30 minutes. Cool.

Frosting:
1 cup brown sugar
3 cups powdered sugar
¼ cup milk
1 teaspoon vanilla
¼ teaspoon maple flavoring
¼ cup black walnuts, finely chopped

Melt the butter on low heat. Add the sugar and milk. Stir for 1 minute. Cool.
Add the powdered sugar and beat the mixture to a spreading consistency. Add in the flavorings, Spread on cake. Sprinkle the top the cake with black walnuts.

Jamaican Rum Cake

1 (18 ½ ounce) box yellow cake mix
1 (3 ¾ ounce) box instant vanilla pudding
4 eggs
½ cup cooking oil
½ cup water
½ cup rum
½ cup chopped pecans

Glaze: ½ cup butter, ¼ cup sugar, ¼ water, and 1-ounce rum

Preheat oven to 325 degrees. Grease and flour a tube pan. Place first 6 ingredients in a large mixing bowl. Using electric mixer, beat 2 minutes, combing well.
Sprinkle pecans on bottom of pan. Pour batter over pecans and bake for 1 hour, or until cake tester comes out clean.

While cake is baking, prepare glaze by combining all ingredients except rum in a small sauce pan and boiling 1 minute. Remove from heat and add rum. When cake is done, remove from oven and pierce top thoroughly with a toothpick.

Immediately pour glaze over top. Cool completely before removing cake from pan. Invert on a serving platter.

David Roberts, Opal Roberts Davidson
&
Ola Roberts Baker

Cocoa Pound Cake

½ pound (2 sticks) butter
1 cup shortening
3 cups sugar
5 eggs
3 cups sifted all- purpose flour
½ teaspoon salt
½ teaspoon baking powder
5 tablespoon cocoa
1 cup milk
1 tablespoon vanilla

Grease and flour bottom of 10- inch tube pan. Cream together butter, shortening, and sugar. Add eggs, one at a time, beating after each. Sift together flour, salt, baking powder, and cocoa. Add to cream mixture alternately with milk and vanilla, beating after each addition. Pour into tube pan. Bake at 325 degrees for 1 hour and 30 minutes or until done. Cool in pan five minutes. Turn out and cool on rack. Frost if desired. This was a recipe from Susie Wadsworth that I made my own.

One Bowl Chocolate Cake

2 cups all-purpose flour
2 cups sugar
½ cup baking cocoa
1 teaspoon baking soda
1 teaspoon baking powder
½ teaspoon salt
1 cup vegetable oil
1 cup buttermilk
2 eggs
1 cup hot water

In a large bowl, combine dry ingredients. Stir in oil, buttermilk, and eggs. Add water and stir until combined. Pour into a greased 13-inch x 9-inch x 2- inch baking pan. Bake at 350 degrees for 35-38 minutes or until a toothpick inserted near the center comes out clean. Cool completely. Frost. Yield 12-16 servings.

Brenda's Southern Comfort Cake

1 package Duncan Hines yellow cake mix
1 package instant vanilla pudding mix
4 eggs
½ cup cold water
½ cup oil
1 cup chopped pecans
½ cup Southern Comfort

Combine cake mix and other ingredients in bowl and beat for 2 minutes. Bake in greased and floured tube or Bundt pan for 1 hour at 325 degrees. Cool 10 minutes; invert on plate. Pierce top of cake with fork. Drizzle and brush top and sides with half glaze. Set other half aside after cake is cooled. Reheat glaze and brush over cake.

Glaze: Melt butter in saucepan. Stir in water and sugar. Boil 3 minutes, stirring constantly. Remove from heat and stir in Southern Comfort.

Fred Mac Sibley, Wayne Sibley, Dale Sibley, Pat Sibley & James Sibley

Italian Cream Cake

½ cup Crisco
1 stick butter
2 cups sugar
2 cups flour
1 tsp. vanilla
Have at room temperature:
5 eggs
1 cup buttermilk
1 teaspoon soda dissolved in buttermilk
1 cup coconut

Cream sugar, Crisco, and butter well; add egg yolks 1 at a time. Beat after each egg. Add flour and milk alternately, beginning with flour. Fold coconut by hand as it sticks to beaters. Fold in stiffly beaten egg whites. Bake in 2 (10-inch) greased cake pans at 350 degrees for 30 minutes. Let cool in pans 5 minutes.

Italian Cream Frosting: 1 stick butter, 1 cup nuts, and 1 (8 oz.) cream cheese. Have butter and cream cheese at room temperature. Sift 1-pound powdered sugar and add gradually to cream mixture.

This recipe was used by Mrs. Margaret Lou Ralston. She would make it each year for our Lord's Acre Auction at Sardis United Methodist Church. Her cake would bring $100 and sometimes as much as $250.

Woman's Day Chocolate Cake

1 ¾ cups flour
1 teaspoon baking soda and salt
1 ½ cup sugar
½ cup shortening
2 eggs
½ cup unsweetened cocoa powder
1 cup hot black coffee
½ cup water

Grease and dust bottom of pans with cocoa, set aside.

In a large bowl cream sugar and shortening until light and fluffy. Add eggs one at a time, beating well.

Dissolve cocoa powder in coffee, stir in water into coffee mixture.

Beat flour mixture with coffee mixture into creamed mixture, beat alternately, until smooth. Pour into prepared pans. Bake in preheated oven 375 degrees for 25 to 30 minutes. *Mother says for her oven she uses 350 degrees.

This cake is very moist. It can be used for cupcakes. This is mother's favorite chocolate cake recipe.

Melvina Craft Roark

Old Fashion Stack Cake

Mix together:

3 ½ cups of flour
1 teaspoon soda
1 cup sugar
½ teaspoon salt
1 teaspoon ginger
½ teaspoon cloves
¾ teaspoon cinnamon
¾ teaspoon nutmeg

Then mix in:

1 stick of butter (1/2 cup)
½ cup molasses
2 eggs slightly beaten
Add ½ cup buttermilk gradually (a little less or more to make a stiff dough.)

Divide dough into six parts. Pat out one part into a greased 9-inch iron skillet or cake pan. Use a little flour on top to help pat in. Bake at 400 degrees for 8 to 10 minutes. Continue baking each of the six parts. Cool.

Filling:

1-pound dried apples
1 cup brown sugar
½ cup white sugar
2 tsp cinnamon
½ teaspoon cloves
½ teaspoon allspice

Cover apples with water. May have to add water to keep apples from sticking to pan. Cook until soft enough to mash. Mash. Add sugars and spices. Cool. Stack cake layers with apple mixture spread between layers. Cover cake and store in refrigerator for 24 hours. This allows for the apple sauce to soak into cake. Can also use apple butter or apple sauce instead of the dried apples.

This recipe came from Aunt Vinia Doyle Roberts. She wrote on the recipe, "I was first introduced to the cake when I was 5. My family and I were visiting my Aunt Melvina Craft Roark. She made a stack cake for my birthday. I remember how everyone talked about how special it was to get a cake with so many layers. It was enjoyed by all. Years later, my cousin, Alene Martin Curry made it for family reunions in Manchester, Kentucky. She gave me this recipe.

The Original Kentucky Whiskey Cake

5 cups flour, sifted
1-pound sugar
1 cup brown sugar
¾ pound butter
6 eggs, separated
2 teaspoons nutmeg
1 teaspoon baking powder
1-pint bourbon
1-pound red candied cherries, cut in pieces or halves
1-pound pecan halves
½ pound golden or white raisins, cut in half-or ½ pound chopped dates
½ pound green candied pineapple, cut up

Soak all the fruits in whiskey overnight.

Cream butter, sugar, and brown sugar until fluffy. Add egg yolks and beat well.

Reserve a small amount of flour for nuts (about a tablespoon). Sift flour, baking powder, and nutmeg together. Add to creamed mixture and mix well.

Beat egg whites until they hold a peak and add slowly to mixture. Add the nuts last.

Bake in a large greased tube pan lined with greased paper in a slow oven (250 to 275 degrees) for 3 to 4 hours.

When cake is cool, store in a tight container. Stuff center hole with cheesecloth which has been soaked in whiskey. Wrap in foil and keep in a very cool place. Wet the cheesecloth again if it dries out.

You can make this cake a month or two ahead of Christmas Day.

Dried Apple Stack Cake

Stack Cake was a traditional Kentucky pioneer wedding cake that was put together right at the wedding celebration. Each woman brought a layer of cake. Applesauce made from fresh or dried apples were spread on each layer, and then the layers were stacked. The last time I went to visit my grandmother, Oda Gay Sizemore, in Bear Branch, Kentucky she had a six-layer Stack Cake sitting on her kitchen table. She would make the cake often. This recipe came from cousin Mildred Woods Roberts.

½ cup shortening
½ cup sugar
1 egg, well beaten
1/3 cup molasses
½ cup buttermilk
3 ½ cups plain flour
½ teaspoon soda
½ teaspoon ginger
1 teaspoon cinnamon
1 teaspoon allspice
1 teaspoon vanilla
Cooked, dried apples (1 pound)

For Apples:
¼ teaspoon cloves
½ teaspoon cinnamon
½ teaspoon allspice
1 cup brown sugar

Cream shortening and sugar. Add beaten eggs, molasses and buttermilk and mix well. Sift flour, soda, ginger, cinnamon and allspice. Make hole in center of dry ingredients. Put in creamed mix and stir until well mixed. Add vanilla. Roll out dough as you would pastry. Cut to fit 9-inch pan. Make about 6 or 7 layers. Bake at 350 degrees for 10 to 20 minutes. Lay on dish towel to cool. Cook apples until soft enough to mash. Let cool. Place first layer on cake plate and add some of the applesauce or dried apples. Continue layering. The last layer will be the cake. Sprinkle top with powdered sugar. Prepare cake at least 1 to 2 days before serving.

Minnie Reed's Raw Apple Cake

2 sticks (1 cup) butter
2 cups sugar
2 large eggs
2-1/2 cup flour
2 tsp. baking powder
1 tsp. soda
½ tsp. salt
2-1/2 cups finely chopped raw apples
1 cup chopped black walnuts

Cream butter and sugar together. Add eggs; beat well. Add the dry ingredients which have been sifted together, then fold in the apples and the nuts thoroughly; the batter will be very stiff. Grease and flour a 13"x9" pan, pour in the batter and smooth it over with a spoon. Bake one hour in a 350 degrees oven. Serve plain or with glaze.

Glaze: 2 cups confectioners' sugar, 1 tablespoon water, 2 tablespoon white syrup, 1 tablespoon soft butter, and 1 tablespoon lemon extract. Just mix all ingredients well and spoon over the warm cake. Serve warm or cold.

This is my mother's recipe. She found the recipe in the Courier Journal several years back.

Grandmother Oda Gay Sizemore & Grandfather Burchel Sizemore

German Apple Cake

2 cups sugar
3 eggs
1 cup butter
1 teaspoon vanilla
2 cups flour
2 teaspoon cinnamon
1 teaspoon salt
1 teaspoon soda
4 cups diced apples
1 cup pecans

Beat together sugar, eggs, butter, and vanilla. Add flour, cinnamon, salt, and soda. Add apples and pecans. Bake in Bundt pan at 350 degrees for 1 hour. Allow to slightly cool and remove from pan. Cool completely before icing.

Icing:
¼ cup butter
1 3-ounce package of cream cheese
2 cups confectioner's sugar
Pecans

Mix all ingredients. Ice cake and top with pecans. Cake is best if made a day ahead to moisten cake.

This recipe came from the "Ripley Bicentennial Cookbook – 1812-2012."

Fruit Cake

1 teaspoon vegetable oil
1 1/3 cups sugar
4 eggs
¼ cup molasses
2 cups Gold Medal flour
1 teaspoon baking powder
2 teaspoon salt
2 teaspoon cinnamon
1 teaspoon nutmeg
1 cup fruit juice
1 cup or more of flour
2 2/3 cups raisins
2 cups cut up dates
2 cups mixed candied fruit
1 cup nuts

Mix oil, sugar, eggs, and molasses. Beat 2 minutes. Blend 2 cups flour, baking powder, salt, and spices together. Stir this into oil mixture. Alternate with fruit juice. Blend extra cup of flour into fruit and nuts. Pour batter over fruit and mix.

Put in greased tube cake pan. Bake at 350 degrees with top of cake covered with waxed paper for about 30 minutes and then remove paper. Bake for about 15 minutes more or until a toothpick comes out clean.

This was a recipe from Aunt Patricia Sauer Roberts. I was only about 10 years old when she married Uncle David. She was such a sweet person. She would let Cleo and I dress up in her clothes. Good memories.

Patricia & David Roberts
with children

German Sweet Chocolate Cake

2 cups white sugar
1 cup Crisco
1 cup buttermilk
4 eggs, separated
2 ½ cups cake flour
1 teaspoon vanilla
1 package German Sweet Chocolate
1 teaspoon soda

Dissolve chocolate in ½ cup boiling water. Beat egg whites until stiff. Cream Crisco and sugar. Add egg yolks that have been beaten. Add ¾ cup buttermilk alternately with flour. Dissolve soda in remaining ¼ cup buttermilk. Add pinch of salt to chocolate and add to the creamed mixture. Add vanilla and fold in egg whites. Bake in 2 (9 or 10-inch) cake pans at 350 degrees.

Frosting:

1 large can Carnation milk
½ cup chopped pecans
1 cup shredded coconut
1 egg
1 cup white sugar
1 stick butter
1 teaspoon vanilla

Mix together and cook until thick, stirring constantly. Spread between layers and over top. This recipe is very old and one of the best. It came from Mary Garvin, a member of the Sardis United Methodist Church when I first started attending in 1970.

Almond Cream Cheese Pound Cake

1 butter recipe golden cake mix
8 oz. cream cheese
4 large eggs
½ cup water
½ cup sugar
½ cup vegetable oil
1 tsp. vanilla
1 ½ tsp. almond extract
Glaze:
1 cup powdered sugar
1 ½ tsp. almond extract
1 to 3 tsp. water

Preheat oven to 350 degrees. Lightly mist and flour a Bundt or tube pan. Place cake mix, cream cheese, eggs, water, sugar, oil, vanilla, and almond extract into a large mixing bowl. Blend on low speed for 1 minute. Increase speed and mix another 2 minutes. Pour into prepared pan. Bake 35 to 40 minutes. Let cool, but while still warm, mix powdered sugar, almond extract and enough water to form a glaze. Remove cake from pan and apply glaze.

Dan Wright would make this cake. He attended Sardis United Methodist Church with Mac and me. He was a wonderful cook.

Ola Roberts Baker & Malvery Roberts Begley

Lou Gibson's Old-Time Gingerbread

8 cups self-rising flour
6 eggs
3 cups brown sugar
12-ounce sorghum (1 ½ cups)
2 sticks soft butter
2/3 cup soft shortening
½ teaspoon soda
3 tablespoons ginger
1 heaping teaspoon allspice

Put all the flour in a bowl. Make a well in center. Put all other ingredients in well. Start working with spoon or hand until all the flour is mixed. Then pinch off a piece of dough about the size of a medium egg. Roll it around in hand to make a ball. Place on ungreased cookie sheet and flatten lighter.

Place six of the gingerbread on a cookie sheet. Bake 15 minutes at 325 degrees. Gingerbread will keep two weeks in a covered container. Dust gingerbread with powdered sugar, if you wish.

This recipe is over 100 years old. This recipe came from Lou Gibson of Hyden, Leslie County, Kentucky. She cooked for the Hyden jail at one time.

This is a recipe that mother started making and now, I guess, we would call it Brenda's recipe. Brenda makes it for the family. She always makes sure that she has it made when I come home. It is my favorite.

Martha Couch's Old Fashion Pan Gingerbread

½ cup buttermilk
½ cup sugar
1 cup sorghum
1 teaspoon salt
1 teaspoon cinnamon
1 teaspoon cloves
1 tablespoon ginger
1 tablespoon soda
2 ½ cups plain flour
2 eggs

Blend all ingredients together. Grease and heat a 13x9-inch pan real hot. Pour in batter. Bake for 40 minutes in 350-degree oven.

This recipe came from Martha Couch. It is a very old recipe. I believe this recipe is more like the gingerbread that Grandma Ida Begley made. It is delicious.

Chocolate-Peanut Butter Amaretto

Crust:
2 cups flour
2 sticks butter
1 cup chopped pecans

With a fork cream butter, flour, and nuts together until it is crumbly. Spread crumbled mixture evenly in greased 9x13 inch baking pan. Bake crust at 350 degrees for about 20 minutes or until golden brown. Let crust cool before filling.

Peanut Butter Layer:
1 (8 ounce) container of frozen non-dairy whipped topping
1 (8 ounce) package cream cheese
½ cup peanut butter
2 tablespoon Amaretto

Cream peanut butter, sugar, and cream cheese together. Add whipped topping and Amaretto and mix with electric mixer until smooth and creamy. Place in cooled crust.

Chocolate Layer:
3 small boxes of instant chocolate pudding
4 ½ cups milk

Mix pudding and milk with mixer at high speed until thick. Spread pudding over peanut butter layer.

Topping:
1 large container of frozen whipped non-dairy topping
½ cup coconut
½ cup chopped pecans

Spread topping over pudding layer and sprinkle with coconut and pecans.

This recipe was one of cousin, Mollie Napier Dezarn. I have made this for church and other events. Serves a lot.

Old Fashion Banana Pudding

1 cup sugar
½ cup all-purpose flour
½ teaspoon salt
2 cups milk (not skim)
4 or 5 ripe bananas sliced thin *cover with plastic wrap or sprinkle with lemon juice to keep them from turning brown
1 box vanilla wafers
1 teaspoon vanilla extract
1 tablespoon butter (not margarine)
4 large egg yolks

Meringue:
4 egg whites, room temperature
5 tablespoon sugar
¼ teaspoon cream of tartar
½ teaspoon vanilla extract

Preheat oven to 375 degrees. Line the bottom of a 9x9 inch pan with a layer of vanilla wafers. Combine sugar, flour, and salt in a bowl, and mix well. Set aside.

In a heavy saucepan, beat the egg yolks well. Over medium heat add the flour mixture to the egg yolks, alternately with the milk and vanilla, stirring constantly. Bring to a gentle boil and, when the mixture begins to thicken, add the butter, continuing to stir. Keep boiling and stirring until mixture reaches a nice pudding consistency. Make sure you don't scorch the pudding. Remove from heat.

Place a layer of banana slices on top of the vanilla wafers. Pour half of the pudding over the banana slices. Put down another layer of vanilla wafers, another layer of banana slices, and cover with remaining pudding.

Beat the egg whites at high speed until they form soft peaks. Add the cream of tartar. At high speed, gradually add the sugar, a tablespoon at a time, and beat until stiff peaks form. Fold the vanilla into meringue, and spread the meringue over the pudding, sealing it at the sides of the dish. Bake until meringue browns, 12 to 15 minutes. Then cool and serve.

This recipe came from a dear friend, Dorothy Baker Osborne, from Booneville, Kentucky. It was a recipe from her mother, Rose Bowling Baker.

Oatmeal Crisps

1-1/2 cup all-purpose flour`
1 tsp. salt
1 tsp. baking soda
1 cup solid vegetable shortening
1 cup packed light brown sugar
½ cup granulated sugar
1 tsp. vanilla
2 eggs
2 cups old-fashioned rolled oats
2 cups raisins

Combine flour, salt, and baking soda. Beat shortening, sugars, and vanilla in large bowl until creamy. Beat in eggs until light and fluffy. Gradually beat in flour mixture and rolled oats. Stir in raisins. Drop by well-rounded teaspoonfuls onto greased baking sheets. Bake in preheated 350 degrees oven for 8 to 10 minutes or until golden brown. Cool cookies on sheets for 2 minutes. Transfer cookies to wire rack to cool.

This is my mother's recipe. I have been baking them for a lot of years. Cousin Maudie Nave Roberts made the cookies and won a blue ribbon at the Grant County, Oklahoma Fair.

Snicker Doodles

Preheat oven 400 degrees.

Mix well: 1 cup shortening, 2 eggs, and 1 ½ cup sugar
Sift and stir in: 2 ¾ cups flour, 2 teaspoons cream of tartar, 1 teaspoon soda, and ½ teaspoon salt

Roll into balls the size of walnuts. Roll in mixture of 4 tablespoons sugar and 4 teaspoons cinnamon. Place 2 inches apart on ungreased cookie sheet. I usually look at them after about 4 or 5 minutes and pat them down just a little. Bake 8-10 minutes until light brown.

Crisp Peanut Butter Cookies

1 cup shortening
1 cup granulated sugar
1 cup brown sugar
1 teaspoon vanilla
2 eggs, beaten
1 cup peanut butter
2 cups sifted all-purpose flour
2 teaspoons soda
1 teaspoon salt

Cream shortening, sugars, and vanilla. Add beaten eggs and beat thoroughly. Stir in peanut butter.

Sift together dry ingredients; stir into creamed mixture. Drop by teaspoons onto ungreased cookie sheets. Press with back of floured fork to make a crisscross design. Bake at 350 degrees, for about 10 minutes, or until lightly browned.
 Yield: About 6 dozen cookies.

This is one of my best recipes. My children (Cindy, Kevin, and Korbin) love me making these cookies for them. I made a batch one day and Korbin ate one. He said, "Grandma, these cookies are bad. So bad I think you shouldn't take them anywhere." I thought he was serious; however, he likes them so much, he doesn't like to share.

Homemade Reese's Bars

2 sticks butter
1 cup peanut butter
1 cup crushed graham crackers
1 box powdered sugar
1 small package chocolate chips

Melt butter in saucepan. Add peanut butter, graham crackers, and sugar. Stir well. The dough will be very stiff. Press dough in a 13x9x2 inch pan, or if you them thinner, on a cookie sheet or jelly roll pan. Melt chocolate chips and spread on top.

I would make these for Cindy when she was young. She is always requesting them.

Coconut Pecan Praline Cookies

2 cups chopped pecans
2 cups sweetened shredded coconut
1 ½ cups sugar
1 cup brown sugar
½ cup evaporated milk
½ cup light corn syrup
½ cup (1 stick) unsalted butter
1 teaspoon salt
1 teaspoon vanilla

1. In a large saucepan over medium high heat, stir together sugars, evaporated milk, corn syrup, and butter until melt melted and smooth.

2. Bring to a boil and cook for 3 minutes, then remove from heat and stir in vanilla extract and salt. Fold in shredded coconut and pecans until incorporated, then continue stirring for 3-4 minutes, or until mixture begins to cool.

3. Once thick, use a tablespoon or small ice cream scoop to drop spoonful of cookies onto wax paper lined baking sheets.

4. Let set completely.

Peanut Blossoms

1 ¾ cups sifted flour
1 teaspoon baking soda
½ teaspoon salt
½ cup shortening
½ cup smooth peanut butter
½ cup sugar
½ cup brown sugar (packed)
1 egg unbeaten
1 teaspoon vanilla
Package of Chocolate Kisses

Sift together flour, soda, and salt. Set aside. Cream shortening with peanut butter. Gradually add sugar creaming well. Blend in unbeaten egg and vanilla. Beat well. Add dry ingredients. Mix well. Shape into balls. Roll in granulated sugar. Remove from oven and press 1 Chocolate Kiss into each cookie. Return to oven 2-5 minutes. Makes 3 dozen.

Mother's Chocolate No-Cook Cookies

2 cups sugars
½ cup cocoa
½ cup milk
1 stick butter
½ cup peanut butter
1 teaspoon vanilla
2 cups Quick Oats
Nuts

Combine sugar, cocoa, milk and butter in a saucepan. Stir and bring to a boil. Cook 1 minute or just a little longer.

Take off stove and stir in remaining ingredients. Drop by spoonful and let stand for 30 minutes before serving.

I remember making these cookies when I was about 12 years old. I have made them all through the years.

Coconut Bon Bon's

1 14-ounce bag of coconut
1 stick butter
1 can Eagle Brand Milk
1-pound (4 cups) confection sugar
½ teaspoon vanilla
Dipping chocolate or 12 oz. bag Chocolate chips
Crisco or paraffin

Mix and chill. Form into balls. Chill again. It will be kind of sticky. Melt chocolate plus a little Crisco or paraffin together. Dip balls into chocolate.

This recipe came from my sister, Brenda.

Old Fashion Sargum Molassie Cookies

1 cup molasses
1 cup sugar
2 eggs
½ cup Crisco
½ teaspoon salt
1 teaspoon ginger
1 teaspoon soda (level)
1 cup buttermilk

Mix molasses, sugar, and eggs together. Add all the other ingredients except Crisco, add Crisco last and make it up with hands as you do biscuits. Add a little more flour if needed, roll out with a dough roller just as you would biscuits. Cut with a biscuit cutter or cookie cutter put in a greased pan. Bake till brown and sprinkle with a little sugar while warm, if desired.

This recipe came from Bernice Campbell and she said it was handed down from her mother, Sophia Treadway. It is an easy recipe but good.

Joe Frogger Cookies

1/3 cup dark rum (such as Myer's brand)
1 tablespoon water
1 ½ teaspoon salt
3 cups all-purpose flour
3/4 teaspoon ground ginger
3/4 teaspoon ground ginger
1/2 teaspoon ground allspice
1/4 teaspoon ground nutmeg
1/8 teaspoon ground cloves
1 cup dark molasses
1 teaspoon baking soda
1/2 cup unsalted butter, softened but still cool
1 cup granulated sugar

In a small bowl, stir together the rum, water and salt until the salt dissolves. In a medium bowl, whisk together the flour, ginger, allspice, nutmeg, and cloves. In a large measuring cup, stir together the molasses and baking soda (the mixture will begin to bubble), and let sit approximately 15 minutes until doubled in volume.

With an electric mixer on medium-high speed, beat together the butter and sugar approximately 2 minutes until fluffy. Reduce the speed to medium-low and gradually beat in the rum mixture. Add the flour mixture and the molasses mixture, alternately in two batches; scraping the sides of the bowl as needed. Cover the bowl with plastic wrap and refrigerate until stiff, at least 8 hours or up to 3 days.

Preheat oven to 375 degrees F. Adjust two oven racks to the upper-middle and lower-middle positions. Line two baking sheets with parchment paper.

Working with half of the cookie dough, which will be soft) at time on a heavily floured work surface, roll out the dough to 1/4-inch thick. Cut out the cookies with a 3- to 3 1/2-inch cookie cutter or the rim of a drinking glass. Space the cut-out cookies 1 1/2-inch apart on the prepared baking sheets (only 6 cookies per baking sheet as they will spread).

Bake approximately 6 to 7 minutes, switching and rotating the baking sheets halfway through baking, or until the cookies are set and just beginning to crack. Remove from the oven and let the cookies cool on the baking sheets for 10 minutes, then transfer to a wire rack to cool completely.

Repeat with the remaining dough using a fresh or cooled baking sheet.

Refrigerated dough stays fresh about a week, frozen dough three months.

The cookies can be stored in an airtight container for up to 1 week. Yield 2 dozen.

Mother's Potato Candy

1 box confectioner's sugar
1 teaspoon butter
1 teaspoon vanilla
1 boiled potato (about the size of an egg)
Peanut butter as needed

Put potato, butter, vanilla into sugar. Mix well. Roll out flat, spread peanut butter on mixture. Roll like jelly roll. Chill well. Slice.

Xmas Cocoa Fudge

½ cup cocoa
3 cups sugar
3 cups peanut butter
1/8 teaspoon salt
1 ½ cup milk
1 teaspoon vanilla
1 cup walnuts, broken in small pieces

In large iron skillet mix sugar, milk, cocoa, and salt. Stir until mixed. Bring mixture to boil on medium heat. Continue until drop in cool water forms a soft ball. Remove from heat, add vanilla and peanut butter. Mix quickly. Pour in buttered pie plate or dish.

This recipe came from cousin, Malvery Roberts Powell. She told me it was her mother's recipe. It was the only candy that they had at Christmas. Her mother was Oda Sizemore Roberts.

Sweet & Salty Delights

40 small pretzel twists
40 Rolo caramels
40 whole pecan halves

Preheat oven to 400 degrees. Spread out pretzel twists on a jelly-roll pan or cookie sheet and place a Rolo on top of each pretzel. Bake for 3 minutes. Remove from oven and press a whole pecan half on each melted Rolo. Let cool and serve.

Mrs. Vasiloff's Nutty Noodles

1- 12 ounces chocolate chips
1- 12 ounces butterscotch chips
8 ounces salted peanuts
1- 6 ounces Chow Mein noodles

Melt chocolate chips and butterscotch chips in top of double boiler. Stir in nuts and noodles until well mixed. Drop teaspoonfuls on wax paper. Keep stored in refrigerator. I make these a lot. The recipe says to keep in refrigerator, but I don't, I just put them in a tin. I have been making these for 30 years, at least. I received the recipe from Sue Sibley. People always like them.

Holiday Chocolate Haystacks

1 cup semisweet chocolate chips
1 cup milk chocolate chips
3 cups Chow Mein noodles
½ cup roughly chopped almonds
½ cup shelled pistachios
2 tablespoon assorted holiday sprinkles

Heat 2 inches of water in a pot to a simmer. Add the semisweet and milk chocolate chips to a bowl and place over the pot of simmering water. Allow to melt, stirring occasionally, 4 to 5 minutes.

Meanwhile, add the noodles, almonds and pistachios to a large bowl and set aside.

When the chocolate has melted completely, pour over the noodle and nut mixture. Mix until everything is well-coated in the melted chocolate.

Drop teaspoonfuls on wax paper. Sprinkle the holiday sprinkles over the top. Allow to dry completely before storing, about 1 hour.

White Chocolate Christmas Haystacks

3 ½ cups Chow Mein noodles
2 ½ cups salted cocktail peanuts
32-ounce white chocolate candy coating
Candy Sprinkles

Melt the white chocolate slowly. Add salted cocktail peanuts and Chow Mein noodles. Sprinkle candy sprinkles over them.

Angie's Bourbon Balls

½ cup chopped pecans
5 tablespoons bourbon
1-pound confection sugar
¼ lb. butter
6 oz. chocolate
1 finger paraffin

Soak pecans in bourbon several hours or overnight. Blend sugar with softened butter. Add nuts and bourbon. Refrigerate until firm enough to shape into balls.
Chill balls overnight. Melt chocolate and paraffin in the top of a double boiler. Dip balls in chocolate and decorate with pecan halves. Place on waxed paper to dry.

This recipe came from cousin, Angie Begley Baker, of Krypton, Kentucky. She is a wonderful cook.

Country House Fudge

4-1/2 cups white sugar
1 teaspoon salt
½ cup butter
1 (12 ounce) can evaporated milk
2 cups semi-sweet chocolate chips
4 (4 ounce) bars Sweet German Chocolate bars
7 ounces chocolate candy bar (Hershey)
1 (7 ounces) jar marshmallow crème
2 teaspoon vanilla extract
4 cups chopped pecans or walnuts

Butter two 9x13 inch pans. Set aside. Into a large bowl, place chocolate chips and broken up chocolate bars. Make a depression in chocolate pieces, then scoop marshmallow crème into it.

In a saucepan, cook sugar, salt, butter, and milk for about 8 to 10 minutes. Start timing after boiling begins. Remove from heat, add vanilla and chopped nuts. Mix rapidly with large wooden spoon. Pour into buttered pans.

See's Fudge

4 cups sugar
1 large can Pet milk
½ pound butter
3 (6 ounce) package chocolate chips
24 large marshmallows
4 cups nutmeats (optional)
1 teaspoon vanilla

Boil sugar and milk 10 minutes (no longer). Last 2 minutes, add butter. Remove from stove; add chocolate chips and stir. Add marshmallows and stir until melted. Add nuts and vanilla. Stir and pour into buttered 9x13 inch pan. Makes 5 pounds.

Million Dollar Fudge

3 (4 ½ ounces) plain Hershey bars
2 (6 ounces) packages chocolate chips
1-pint marshmallow crème
1 tablespoon butter
1-pound pecans (2 cups)
1 teaspoon vanilla
4 ½ cups sugar
1 tall can evaporated milk

Mix the following in a 4-6-quart container. Hershey bars (broken into pieces), chocolate chips, vanilla, marshmallow crème, and butter.

Mix the following in a large heavy pot; sugar and evaporated milk. Let sugar and milk come to a boil. Let boil for 8 minutes. Pour the hot mixture over the chocolate mixture and blend until smooth. Add nuts. Pour into buttered large buttered pan.

This is the recipe I use most often when making Chocolate fudge.

Mamie Eisenhower's Fudge

2 pounds granulated sugar
4 tablespoons butter
Pinch of salt
1 can evaporated milk
12 ounces semi-sweet chocolate chips
12 ounces German Sweet Chocolate
2 squares bitter chocolate
1-pint marshmallow crème

Combine sugar, butter, milk and salt. Stirring constantly, bring to a boil, and boil for 6 minutes.

Melt chocolate in double boiler. Combine sugar mixture, chocolate and marshmallow in large mixing bowl. Beat well with electric beater. Pour in 9x13x2 inch greased pan and let stand 2 to 3 pounds before cutting. Yield 2 pounds.

Hershey's Fudge

1-1/3 cup cocoa
6 cups sugar
1/4 tsp. salt
3 cups milk
1/2 cup butter
2 tsp. vanilla

Combine cocoa, sugar, and salt in a large saucepan. Add milk gradually, mix, bring to a "bubbly" boil on high heat, stirring constantly. Reduce to medium and continue to boil without stirring until it reaches 232 degrees. Remove from heat and add butter and vanilla. DO NOT STIR. Allow fudge to cool at room temperature until it reaches 110 degrees. Beat by hand with mixer until fudge thickens and loses its gloss. Quickly pour in buttered container. Yield 6 pounds.

Unusual Fudge

4 cups sugar
1 cup butter
1-pint marshmallow crème
1 ½ cups pecans
1 tall can milk
1 (12 ounces) package semi-sweet chocolates
1 teaspoon vanilla

Butter sides of large heavy saucepan. Combine sugar, milk, and butter. Cook over medium heat to soft-ball stage, stirring often. This is about 8 minutes. Remove from heat. Add chocolate and marshmallow crème, vanilla, and nuts. Beat until chocolate has melted and pour in buttered pan.

Peppermint Fudge

2-1/2 cups sugar
½ cup butter
1 (5 ounce) can evaporated milk
8 ounces vanilla chips
1 (7 ounces) jar marshmallow crème (2 cups)
½ cup peppermint candy, finely crushed
1 teaspoon peppermint extract

In a heavy large saucepan, combine sugar, butter, and milk. Stir with a wooden spoon but do not turn on the heat yet because I first get all my ingredients and pan ready.

In a large bowl add the jar of marshmallow crème, vanilla chips, peppermint candy and peppermint extract. Have your mixer ready to use.

Butter 8"x8" pan.

Then turn on the stove on medium heat. Stir constantly, the sugar, butter, and milk mixture. You can see it get creamy. When you see the mixture beginning to boil (not heavy-just boiling up) stir for 4-5 minutes. Take off stove and pour the hot mixture into the marshmallow crème, vanilla chips, peppermint candy, and peppermint extract. Use your hand mixer to blend well. Then take a wooden spoon and stir-use heavy strokes to get air into the candy mixture.

Pour into buttered pan. Garnish with Peppermint candy. Place in cool place.

One day my son-in-law, Kevin, came and asked me if I could duplicate the peppermint fudge, he had bought. I tried about four times and finally came up with this recipe. It is very good.

Peanut Butter Fudge

3 cups sugar
2/3 cup butter
1 teaspoon vanilla
1 small can Carnation evaporated milk (5.33 ounces)
1 small jar Kraft marshmallow crème
1 cup peanut butter

Mix 3 cups sugar, 1 small can Carnation evaporated milk and 2/3 cup of butter. Pour in a heavy saucepan and bring to a rolling boil. Let boil for 5 minutes, stirring.

Add 1 small jar of Kraft marshmallow crème, 1 teaspoon vanilla, and 1 cup of peanut butter. Blend together with mixer until creamy. Pour on buttered cookie sheet. Let cool and cut.

At Christmas I make about 30 pounds of this fudge to give out as gifts. It is delicious.

Black Walnut Fudge

3/4 cup margarine
12 ounces white baking chips
3 cups sugar
7 ounces marshmallow crème
2/3 cup evaporated milk
1 teaspoon vanilla
1 teaspoon Black Walnut flavoring
1 cup Black Walnuts

Mix margarine, sugar, and milk in heavy 2 1/2-quart saucepan; bring to full boil, stirring constantly. Continue boiling 5 minutes over medium heat or until candy thermometer reaches 234 degrees F., stirring constantly; remove from heat. Gradually stir in chips until melted; add remaining ingredients and mix well. Pour into greased 9X13 inch pan. Cool at room temperature; cut into squares. Yields 3 pounds.

Date Loaf Candy

1 cup cream
3 cups sugar
1 – 16 ounces package of dates, roughly chopped *Medjool dates are the best
1 tablespoon Karo
1 cup chopped nuts

Stir sugar, cream, dates. Cook over low heat. When it coats the spoon and is foamy it is done. Remove from heat and beat it until it is creamy. Add nuts and beat some more. Roll in a damp cloth and put in the refrigerator. When chilled, remove and sprinkle with powdered sugar.

This is a very old recipe. Very good.

Kentucky Cream Candy

2 cups whipping cream (1 pint)
6 cups sugar (3 pints)
1 cup boiling water
Pinch salt
Pinch soda-could be left out
Butter to butter slab

Measure sugar and pour in enamel kettle. Measure cream add to sugar and stir with wooden spoon. Bring water to boil, pour and stir into cream and sugar mixture. Dissolve soda in small amount of cream left in measuring cup. Add pinch of salt. Add dissolved soda.

Place candy thermometer in kettle, do not let end touch bottom of kettle. Place kettle on medium heat and stir continually until sugar is dissolved or until mixture comes to a full boil. Cook until temperature on thermometer reaches 260 degrees, hard boil.

Butter marble slab, butter slab before cooking time is completed.

When temperature reaches 260 degrees, remove thermometer and place in a glass of hot water. This is to melt candy from thermometer.

Quickly pour mixture unto buttered slab. Fill kettle with hot water to clean quickly.

Butter hands, turn edges of candy up into middle of candy, roll candy together and start pulling.

If too hot to pull, keep moving around on slab and keep slab buttered.

Best results for cutting, stretch small amount the length of slab for someone to cut while pulling so candy will not get to hard to cut. Continue until all is cut.

This recipe is from Celia Bowling. Kentucky Cream Candy is an old-time recipe that goes back to at least the early 1900's or before.

Canning & Preserving

Fred Mac & Linda Sibley with children: Kevin, Cindy, and Korbin Thayer

Mustang Grape Jelly

Wash grapes, thoroughly; the stems need not be removed. Place washed grapes in a cooker and add enough water to cover them; after the grapes and water start to boil, cook stirring frequently until the skins begin to pop. When the skins slip easily from the grapes, they are ready to press. Strain the cooked grapes and juice through a colander.

Place 5 cups of strained juice and add a box of pectin, a tablespoon of butter, and a tablespoon of lemon juice in a heavy pot. Stir and let sit for a minute or so. Then cook on medium high heat. Let cook until boiling. Boil for 1 or 2 minutes. Then add 7 cups of sugar. Stir well and let it come back to a boil. Boil for 5 minutes. Then place in washed and warm canning jars, cleaning well the lids and rings. Then place in canner. Let boil for 5-10 minutes.

Be careful with the mustang grapes. They are bitter to eat and can irritate the skin due to a high acid content. You should use gloves; however, I cannot do anything wearing gloves.

Pomegranate Jelly

3 ½ cups pomegranate juice
1 package (1 ¾ ounce) powdered fruit pectin
1 tablespoon lemon juice
1 tablespoon butter
5 cups sugar

In a Dutch oven, combine pomegranate juice, pectin, lemon juice, and butter. Stir and let stand for 1 or 2 minutes. Cook over medium high heat. Bring to a full rolling boil, stirring constantly. Stir in sugar; return to a full rolling boil. Boil for 2 minutes, stirring constantly. Remove from heat; skim off foam, if any. Pour hot liquid into hot sterilized half pint jars; leaving ¼ inch headspace. Wipe rims and adjust lids. Process for 5 minutes in a boiling water canner.

I make Pomegranate Jelly each year for the Lord's Acre Auction at our church. I never bring home a jar.

Sand Plum (Wild Plum) Jelly

5 ½ cup plum juice
1 tablespoon lemon juice
¼ cup lemon juice
6 ½ cup sugar (measure into separate bowl)
1 box Sure Jell Pectin

Wash plums well. Then place in a large heavy cooker with a little water. Mash plums and let cook. Cool and use cheese cloth or towel to strain juice.

Mix juice and pectin in heavy large pot. Add ½ teaspoon butter and 1 tablespoon of lemon juice. Let sit for 1-2 minutes. Place on stove and bring mixture to a full rolling boil on high heat, stirring constantly. Boil for 1 minute.

Stir in sugar quickly. Return to full rolling boil and boil exactly 1 minute, stirring constantly. Remove from heat. Skim off any foam with a metal spoon. Ladle quickly into prepared jars, filling to with 1/8 inch of top. Wipe jar rims and threads. Cover with flat lids. Then screw bands tightly. Place in hot water bath for approximately 5 minutes. Then let cool.

Sand plums grow wild in the southern United States from Texas and Oklahoma eastward. They are also called sand hill plums or Chickasaw plums. The tree often forms thickets of plants only a few feet tall. It is a small red-orange plum.

We don't have sand plum trees on our farm. I go to visit my cousin Jimmy Roberts in Pond Creek, Grant County, Oklahoma. He has a farm and lots of sand plum trees. Making the sand plum jelly isn't cheap, but so good. People love it.

Cherry Preserves

6 cups cherries
1 package powdered fruit pectin
1 tablespoon lemon juice
1 tablespoon butter

Coat the above with ½ cup of sugar. Let stand for a few minutes. Then cook; stirring often. You can mash the cherries down; however, I like mine to stay whole, as much as possible. Let come to a boil for about 2-5 minutes. Add 3 cups sugar. Bring to boil again for 1 minute or a little more. Remove from heat. Pour hot mixture into hot sterilized jars, leaving ¼ inch headspace. Wipe rims and adjust lids. Process for 5 minutes in a boiling water canner.

Brenda's Crock Pot Apple Butter

6-7 apples (18 cups) or 1 pound is equal to 3 cups sliced
½ cup sugar
1 cup brown sugar
2 teaspoons cinnamon
½ teaspoon nutmeg
¼ teaspoon cloves
¼ teaspoon salt
1 tablespoon vanilla

Wash, peel, slice apples very thin. Combine other ingredients except vanilla. Pour over apples and mix well. Put in a large crockpot and fill it to the top.

Cook on high for 5 hours. Stir occasionally and it will reduce to half. Pour in vanilla, cook covered 1 hour or until desired consistency. Use a whisk to mash/stir. Ladle into hot jars. 1 ¼ head space. Process jars for 15 minutes. Makes 6 half-pint jars.

Chow Chow

2 gallons green tomatoes
2 stalks celery
6 large onions
6 medium sweet green pepper
1 medium firm cabbage head or less
1 cup hot pepper
4 or 5 cups sugar
½ cup salt
Pickling spice

Chop all the above in medium small pieces, place in large cooking container. Cover with apple cider vinegar. Heat until it changes color from dark green, do not boil-simmer only. Fill jars while hot and seal well. Let set at least 6 weeks.

This recipe was one of Grandmother Martha Ann Pritchard Sibley. After she died her husband, Grandfather Emerson, would make Chow Chow and give to the family. Then we begin to make it.

Canning Tomatoes

1. Set out all equipment and utensils needed. Fill large saucepan 2/3 full of hot water; place on high heat to boil.
2. Carefully examine jars for nicks, cracks, or sharp edges on sealing surface.
3. Wash jars and closures in hot soapy water. Rinse well.
4. Wash tomatoes carefully and drain.
5. Put tomatoes in wire basket and lower into boiling water in the saucepan. Remove after about 30 seconds or as soon as skin starts to crack. Dip into cold water.
6. Cut out core, removed skins and trim of any green spots. Drop whole tomato into jar. Large tomatoes should be cut into quarters.
7. Press tomatoes in jar. Fill to ½ inch of the top.
8. Add 1 teaspoon canning salt to each quart. Run a non-metallic kitchen knife between tomatoes and jar to release any trapped air bubbles.
9. Wipe top and threads of jar with clean damp cloth.
10. When jars are filled, stand each on rack in canner of hot, not boiling, water.
11. Cover. Bring water to boil. Process quarts 45 minutes.

This recipe was written down one day when I was canning tomatoes at my mother's farm. Mother didn't have a recipe, so I wrote it down as I did the canning. It was a wonderful day.

Pickled Peaches

1 cup cider vinegar
1 cup water
2 cups sugar
1 teaspoon ground cloves
1-quart peaches peeled
6 whole cloves
2 cinnamon sticks

Combine vinegar, water, sugar, and ground cloves in a stainless-steel pan and boil for 10 minutes. Add peaches to the syrup and cook for 15 minutes or until tender.
Pack peaches in 2-pint jars and add cloves and a cinnamon stick to each jar. Fill jars with syrup. Seal and process in a boiling water bath for 20 minutes.

Strawberry-Rhubarb Jam

4 cups fresh strawberries crushed
2 cups chopped rhubarb
1 tablespoon butter
¼ cup lemon juice
1 package (1 ¾ ounce) powdered fruit pectin
5 ½ cups sugar

In a Dutch oven, combine the strawberries, rhubarb, butter, and lemon juice. Stir in pectin. Let sit for a minute or 2. Place on stovetop and bring to a full rolling boil, stirring constantly. Stir in sugar, return to a full rolling boil. Boil for 1 minute, stirring constantly.

Remove from the heat. Skim off foam. Carefully ladle hot mixture into hot sterilized pint jar, leaving ¼-inch head space. Process for 5 minutes in a boiling water canner.

Green Tomato Pickles

7 quarts green tomatoes sliced thin
1 cup sliced hot pepper
5 large onions sliced thin

Mix together:
½ cup canning salt
4 cups sugar
4 cups vinegar

Pour this over vegetable. Cook over medium heat, stirring gently until vegetables change color. Pack and seal. Makes about 12 pints. I cold pack mine for about 15 minutes after water begins to boil to make them have a good seal.

Pepper Jelly

2 red peppers, seeded, finely chopped (about 1 ½ cups)
2 green peppers, seeded, finely chopped (about 1 ½ cups)
10 large jalapeno peppers, seeded, finely chopped (1/2 pound or about 1 cup)
1 cup Heinz Apple Cider Vinegar
1 package Sure-Jell Fruit Pectin
½ teaspoon butter
5 cups sugar measured into separate bowl

Bring boiling-water canner, half-full of water, to simmer. Wash jars and screw bands in hot soapy water; rinse with warm water. Pour boiling water over flat lids in saucepan off the heat. Let stand in hot water until ready to use. Drain well before filling.

Place peppers in 6-8-quart saucepot. Add vinegar. Stir in pectin. Add butter to reduce foaming. Bring mixture to full rolling boil (a boil that doesn't stop bubbling when stirred) on high heat, stirring constantly. Stir in sugar. Return to full rolling boil and boil exactly 1 minute, stirring constantly. Remove from heat. Skim off any foam with metal spoon.

Ladle immediately into prepared jar, filling to within ¼ inch of tops. Wipe jar rims and threads. Cover with 2-piece lids. Screw bands tightly. Place jars on elevated rack in canner. Lower rack into canner. (Water must cover jars by 1 to 2 inches. Add boiling water, if necessary). Cover; bring water to gentle boil. Process 10 minutes. Remove jars and place upright on towel to cool completely. After jars cool, check seals by pressing centers of lids with finger. (If lid springs back, lid is not sealed, and refrigeration is necessary.)

This is sister Brenda's recipe. She makes the jelly and shares.

Elderberry Jelly

3 cups Elderberry juice
1/4 cup fresh, strained lemon juice
4-1/2 cup sugar
1 package powdered fruit pectin

Clean and remove the stems from the elderberries and place in a large kettle. Crush berries, cover and let simmer for about 15 minutes. Strain juice through a piece of cheesecloth. Measure juice making sure you have 3 cups into a heavy kettle. Stir in lemon juice and pectin into the kettle. Bring mixture to full rolling boil over high heat, stirring constantly. Stir in the sugar quickly. Return to full rolling boil and boil for exactly 1 minute, stirring constantly. Remove from heat and skim off any foam with spoon. Ladle hot mixture quickly into prepared jars, filling to with 1/8 inch of tops. Clean jar rims. Place the lids on tightly and process for 5 minutes in boiling water bath. This will make about 5 cups of the best jelly you can make.

Apricot Jam

5 cups of apricots
¼ cup lemon juice
1 tablespoon butter
7 cups sugar measured to separate bowl
1 box Sure-Jell

Finely chop unpeeled apricots. Measure 5 cups prepared fruit into large heavy pot. Stir in lemon juice. Stir in pectin. Add butter. Let sit for 1 or 2 minutes.

Place on stove and bring mixture to full rolling boil, stirring constantly. Stir in sugar. Bring to another full rolling boil and boil 1 minute or so, stirring constantly. Remove from heat. Ladle immediately into prepared jars. Place in hot water bath for approximately 5 minutes. Then let cool.

Fig Jam

5 cups Fig
½ cup lemon juice
½ cup water
7 cups sugar
1 box (1.75 ounces) Sure-Jell Fruit Pectin
1 teaspoon butter

Bring boiling-water canner, half full of water, to simmer. Wash jars and screw bands in hot soapy water. Rinse them with warm water. Pour boiling water over flat lids in saucepan, sitting off the heat. Let jars and lids stand in hot water until ready to use. Drain jars well before filling.

Trim stems end from figs, finely chop or grind fruit. Measure exactly 5 cups prepared fruit into large heavy saucepan. Stir in lemon juice and water. Stir in pectin. Add butter to reduce foaming. Let sit for 1 minute or so. Place on medium-high heat, stirring constantly. Stir in sugar. Return to full rolling boil and boil exactly 1 minute, stirring constantly. Remove from heat. Skim off any foam with metal spoon. Ladle immediately into prepared jars, filling to with 1/8 inch of tops. Wipe jar rims and threads. Cover with two-piece lids. Screw bands tightly. Place jars on elevated rack in canner. Lower rack into canner. Water must cover jars by 1 to 2 inches-add boiling water if needed. Cover, and bring water to gentle boil. Boil for 10 minutes, then remove jars and place upright on a towel to cool completely.

After jars cool, check seals by pressing middles of lids with finger. If lids spring back, lids are not sealed, and refrigeration is necessary.

Fig Strawberry Preserves

3 cups of mashed figs
3 cups of sugar
1 large box of Strawberry Jell-O

Wash whole figs in sink full of water. Cut off the stems and the bad spots
Mash the figs with the potato masher and add sugar and Jell-O. Stir and cook on medium/high heat until boiling. The mixture will turn deep red. This takes about 20-25 minutes. It is done when a drop of the liquid hangs off the edge of the spoon.
Using a funnel, ladle into hot sterile canning jars, top with hot sterile lids, and seal with rings. Process in a boiling water bath for 15 minutes.

I made these preserves for Lord's Acre this year. I am not a big fan of figs and I had a lot, so this was just another way to prepare them. I had comments from some friends that they really liked them. So, will continue to make, as they are so easy.

Polk Stalk Pickles

To pickle Polk stalk, use only tender stalks not over 6 inches high. Cut into 3-inch lengths. Trim off leaves. Cook in clear water for about 5 minutes. Discard water. Cover again with salted water and boil for about another 5 minutes. Discard water. Pack stalks vertically in jars. Cover with this solution: To each pint of vinegar add ½ teaspoon mustard seed and 2 tablespoons sugar. Heat to boiling, pour over pickles and seal.

Old-Fashioned Whole Fig Preserves

12 cups whole figs
4 cups water
6 cups sugar
4 slices of lemon-seeds removed
Pinch of salt

Wash figs in cool water. Remove stems. Boil a saucepan of water, gently place figs in and remove from heat. Let sit 3 minutes and then drain quickly.

In a heavy-bottomed pot, combine sugar and water and bring to a rolling boil, stirring constantly until it makes a clear syrup. Do not burn.

Add lemon slices, and then gently place figs into boiling liquid. Lower heat to medium and cook figs for about 2 ½ hours, or until figs seem soft. During the cooking process, swirl the pot to stir rather than using a spoon to keep from breaking the figs.

Once figs are done cooking, place funnel on top of hot jar. Using a slotted spoon, gently fill hot jar with figs, slice of lemon, and then ladle hot syrup over figs, leaving ¼ inch head space.

Wipe edge with clean cloth, removing any syrup from rim that would prevent a solid seal. Now, put on a lid, then a band, and using a hot pad, screw the band on tight.

Do one jar at a time until the preserves are used. Process in a boiling water bath for ten minutes.

This recipe takes a long time and you must watch your pot, so you do not overcook the figs or the syrup. If you have your heat too high, you will get a "candied" result rather than a spreadable preserve.

Candied Jalapenos/ Cowboy Candy

3 pounds fresh, firm jalapeno peppers washed
2 cups cider vinegar
6 cups white granulated sugar
1/2 teaspoon turmeric
1/2 teaspoon celery seed
3 teaspoons granulated garlic
1 teaspoon ground cayenne pepper

Instructions:
1. Remove the stems from all the jalapeno peppers.
2. Slice the peppers into uniform 1/8-1/4- inch rounds. Set aside
3. In a large pot, bring the cider vinegar, white sugar, turmeric, celery seed, granulated garlic, and cayenne pepper to a boil. Reduce heat and simmer for **5 minutes.** Add the peppers slices and bring to boil. Then reduce heat and simmer for **4 minutes**. Use a slotted spoon to transfer the peppers and loading into clean, sterile canning jars, within 1/4 inch of the upper rim of the jar. Turn heat up under the syrup and bring to a full rolling boil. Boil hard for **6 minutes**.
4. Use a ladle to pour the boiling syrup into the jars over the jalapeno slices. Insert a knife to the bottom of the jar two or three times to release any trapped pockets of air. Adjust the level of the syrup if necessary. Wipe the rims of the jars with a clean damp paper towel and fix on new two-piece lids.
5. Place jars in a canner, cover with water by 2 inches. Bring the water to a full rolling boil. When it reaches a full rolling boil, set the timer for 10 minutes for half-pints or 15 minutes for pints. When completed transfer the jars to a cooling rack. Leave them to cool for 24 hours. When fully cooled wipe them with a clean damp washcloth then label.
6. Allow to mellow for at least two weeks, but preferably a month before eating.
7.*If you have leftover syrup, it may be canned. It's wonderful brushed on meat on the grill or added to potato salad.

This is sister Brenda's recipe.

Grandmother's Salt Pickles

Combine: 1-quart vinegar, 1-pint water, and ½ cup pickling salt. Bring to a hard boil. Gather cucumbers when small. Leave stems on them. Wash and pack in jars. Pour vinegar and salt solution over cucumbers and seal. This solution makes enough for 3 or 4 quarts of pickles. You may put a small bunch of dill in each jar, if you wish.

Pickled Okra

Wash: 4 pounds small tender okra. Pack in hot sterilized jars. Place in each jar: 1 pod hot red pepper, 1 garlic clove, and sprig of dill (if desired). Heat to boiling point: 1 cup water, 8 cups pure vinegar, ¾ cup pickling salt (not iodized). Pour hot mixture over okra and seal.

*Do not use for 8 weeks. Okra will be crisp and delicious.

Pickled Sweet Onions

8 cups thinly sliced sweet onions
2 tablespoon canning salt
1 ¾ cups white vinegar
1 cup sugar
1 teaspoon dried thyme

Place onions in a colander over a plate, sprinkle with canning salt and toss. Let stand for 1 hour. Rinse and drain onions, squeezing to remove excess liquid.
In a Dutch oven, combine vinegar, sugar and thyme; bring to a boil. Add onions and return to a boil. Reduce heat; simmer, uncovered, 10 minutes. Remove from heat.

Carefully ladle hot mixture into hot half-pint jars, leaving ½ inch headspace. Remove air bubbles, wipe rims and adjust lids. Process for 10 minutes in a boiling water canner.

Pickled Beets

2 cups vinegar
1 cup water
1 cup sugar
Small beets
1 pinch pickling spices

Wash beets. Cover with water and cook until tender. Peel and slice. Mix together vinegar, water, and sugar. Stir and heat until sugar dissolved. Pour this mixture over beets and heat to boiling. Fill jars, then add a pinch of pickling spice to each jar and seal.

I enjoy making pickled beets. They have such a pretty color and look beautiful in jars. My son-in-law could eat a jar in one meal.

Refrigerator Pickles

Mix:
1-gallon sliced cucumbers
1-quart onions
2 tablespoons of pickling salt
Let set for 2 hours. <u>Do not add any water</u>.
Mix:
3 cups sugar
1 cup vinegar
Pour over cucumbers and onions. Let set for 2 hours. Fill jars. Tighten lids and store in refrigerator.

This recipe is from my grandmother, Oda Gay Sizemore. My sister, Velma, and most of the grandchildren called her Maw.

Tole Roberts' Kraut

Chop cabbage up, put in quart jar, half full, level teaspoon full of canning salt, fill jar up to top of jar, cram cabbage in jar, then another level spoon of canning salt. Pour hot water in the jar until water comes to top, lid on and hand tighten. Put in dark place. Do not use water that has been treated with chemicals, like city or county water. You can put a pod of hot pepper in the bottom if you want too, if you like it hot.

Cousin John Roberts makes this Kraut. Mother says it is the best and easiest way to make Kraut.

John Roberts and daughter, Stephanie

This & That

Linda Roberts Sibley

Cornmeal Gravy

¼ to ½ cup grease from bacon or fatback, or lard
1 cup cornmeal
3 cups milk or half milk and half water

Get the grease really hot and add the cornmeal. Stir until the cornmeal is brown. Stir in your water or milk and stir constantly until it is thick. Salt and pepper to taste. Mother adds a little flour to the cornmeal.

Tomato Gravy

2 tablespoons butter
2 tablespoons minced shallots or onion
1 (14 ½ ounce) can diced tomatoes, undrained
½ cup whipping cream
1 teaspoon chicken bouillon granules
½ teaspoon sugar
¼ teaspoon pepper

Melt butter in a large skillet over medium heat; add shallots, and sauté until tender. Stir in whipping cream and remaining ingredients; simmer, stirring often, 3 minutes or until mixture is thickened. Yield: 2 cups. Mother's recipe.

Mother's Red-Eye Gravy

After frying slices of country ham, drain off excess fat. Add a little water to the drippings and a little coffee (if you wish). Cook and stir for a few minutes. Pour into dish around ham. Serve.

I like my red eye gravy poured over regular pan gravy which has been put on a biscuit.

Chocolate Gravy

3 tablespoon flour
3 tablespoon cocoa
1 cup sugar (sweeten to taste)
2 cups water

Bring water to boil. Mix flour and chocolate with a little water or milk in a bowl. Pour into boiling water. Stir, then take it off the stove and sweeten to taste. Serve over hot biscuits.

Confectioners' Frosting

½ cup shortening (white Crisco)
3 cups sifted powdered sugar
4 to 5 tablespoon milk
1 teaspoon vanilla
½ teaspoon almond flavoring
Food coloring, if desired

Mix ingredients with mixer until well blended and it is the right texture to spread. Food coloring of your choice may be added.

Maudie's Glazed Pecans

1 cup sugar
½ cup water
1 tsp. cinnamon
¼ tsp. allspice
2 cups pecans
1 tsp. vanilla (last) after cooking

Combine sugar, water, cinnamon, and allspice in large pan. Cook on medium heat for 5 minutes, stirring constantly. Add pecans. Continue cooking and stirring another 5 minutes. Remove from heat and stir in vanilla. Place pecans individually on waxed paper. Cool completely.

Sugared Pecans

2 cups sugar
1 cup evaporated milk
1 teaspoon vanilla
6 cups pecans

Boil sugar in milk, until it forms a soft ball when dropped into cold water. Add vanilla just before it reaches this stage. Stir in pecans and coat well. Spoon onto waxed paper or brown paper and separate.

Chiles Gureos Rellenos y Asados

Yellow peppers, 2 or 3 per person
Oaxaca or Asadero cheese or Queso Fresco

Cut the chilies open lengthwise. With the help of a spoon, carefully scrape out the veins and seeds. Stuff the chilies with lots of cheese. If you're worried that the cheese will fall out, you can close the chilies and secure with a toothpick. Roast the chilies on the grill or Comal over a low flame, turning occasionally until the cheese has completely melted and the chilies are tender. Remove the chilies from the heat and transfer to a heatproof plate. Serve with Carne Asada, cooked beans, and Mexican rice.

This recipe came from my long-time housekeeper Yolanda Martinez.

Amish Church Peanut Butter Spread

3 pounds crunchy or smooth peanut butter
2 quarts light Karo
2 quarts marshmallow topping

Mix until smooth. Add more Karo if too thick.

French Toast

1 cup milk
1 egg, beaten
1 tablespoon sugar
1 teaspoon vanilla
Slices white bread

Mix all ingredients except bread. Dip bread into milk mixture and fry on both sides in a cast-iron skillet in shortening until golden brown.

Lemon Dressing

1 egg
1 tablespoon water
½ cup sugar
1 tablespoon flour
½ cup lemon juice

Use small saucepan with thick bottom. Beat egg with water. Mix sugar with flour and add to egg mixture. Add lemon juice. Cook slow over medium heat. Stir constantly until thick. Pour over sliced bananas. This is good over most cut fruits. It will keep for a week in refrigerator.

Framboise (Raspberry) Sauce

1 half-pint package fresh raspberries
1/2 cup granulated sugar
1/4 cup water
1 cup (12-ounce seedless raspberry jam)
1 Tsp. Framboise liqueur

Place the package of raspberries, the granulated sugar, and 1/4 cup water in a small saucepan. Bring to a boil, lower the heat, and simmer for 4 minutes. Pour the cooked raspberries, the jam, and Framboise into the bowl of a food processor fitted with the steel blade and process until smooth. Chill.

I order the Framboise liqueur from Amazon. I make this and spoon over a white cake. Beautiful and so good.

Mayan Salsa Habanero Sauce

1 large red onion, finely diced
6 large tomatoes, finely diced
1 bunch chopped cilantro
3 cloves garlic minced
4 Habanero chilies minced
2 tablespoons vinegar
1 tablespoon orange juice
1 tablespoon salt

Mix all ingredients together in a bowl. Cover and refrigerate for up to 3 days. Use with chips as a simple dip or as a condiment to any Mexican dish.

This is another recipe from my long-time housekeeper Yolanda Martinez.

Bourbon Cranberries

2 packages (12 ounce each) fresh or frozen cranberries, thawed
1 ½ cups sugar
1 cup orange juice
¼ cup bourbon
3 teaspoon vanilla extract
1 teaspoon grated orange peel

In a large saucepan, combine the cranberries, sugar, orange juice and bourbon. Bring to a boil. Reduce heat; simmer, uncovered, for 18-22 minutes or until berries pop and mixture has thickened.

Stir in vanilla and orange peel. Carefully ladle hot mixture into hot half-pint jars, leaving ¼ inch headspace. Remove air bubbles; wipe rims and adjust lids. Process for 15 minutes in a boiling-water canner.

I like to make gifts for my friends during the holidays. This is a great gift.

Florence Begley Cochran's Popcorn Balls

¾ cup brown sugar
¾ cup white sugar
½ cup water
½ cup molasses (sorghum)
¼ cup butter
1 tablespoon vinegar
½ tsp. soda
Fresh popped corn

Put sugars in a sauce pan with the molasses, water and vinegar. Cook until it spins a thread, and then add the butter until the hard ball stage is reached when some is dropped into cold water. Add soda and remove from heat.

Have corn freshly popped in a large pan. Pour the syrup over it. Wet hands and press into size desired.

This recipe is from Florence Begley Cochran. She said the recipe is close to how her mother, Nancy Margaret Wooton Begley, made it. Her mother never had a written recipe.

Tommie Worthy's Caramel Pecans

3 cups untoasted pecans
½ cup brown sugar
¼ cup light corn syrup
4 tablespoons (1/2 stick) butter, cut into pieces
¼ teaspoon salt
¼ teaspoon baking soda
¼ teaspoon cinnamon
¼ teaspoon vanilla

1. Place the pecans in a 9x13 pan and set aside. Preheat the oven to 250 degrees.
2. Combine the brown sugar, corn syrup, butter, and salt in a medium saucepan over medium high heat. Stir until the sugar melts and bring it to a boil.
3. Boil the mixture, without stirring for 4 minutes. Once the 4 minutes is up, remove immediately from the heat. Add the vanilla, cinnamon, and baking soda and stir quickly.
4. Immediately pour the mixture over the pecans in the pan and stir to coat the pecans thoroughly.
5. Bake the caramel pecans for 40 minutes, stirring after every 10 minutes.
6. Remove the pecans from the oven and spoon them into a baking sheet covered with foil. Allow them to cool at room temperature, and once cool, break them into pieces. Store caramel pecans in an airtight container or Ziploc bag at room temperature.

Index of Recipes

Beverages & Appetizers

Aunt Janie's Tangy Vegetable Dip	11
Bean Dip	15
Beth's Artichoke Dip	12
Betsy's Wassail	10
Bev's Chicken Luncheon Salad	17
Bourbon Frankfurters	12
Buffalo Chicken Dip	14
Café Au Lait	7
Chili-Cheese Dip	14
Cindy's Tortilla Rolls	15
Cranberry Wreath Punch	7
Cucumber Sandwiches	15
Dove's Nest Almond Bacon Cheddar Spread	13
Dove's Nest Eggnog	7
Dove's Nest Orange Spiced Iced Tea	6
Ed Leach's Hot Wieners	13
Extension Service Punch	8
Frosty Wedding Punch	9
Fruit Slush	7
Homemade Hot Chocolate	8
Hot Spicy Punch	9
Kentucky Benedictine Spread	16
Kentucky Punch Recipe	8
Linda's Dip	11
Mexican Corn Dip	11
Old-Fashioned Lemonade	10
Pimento Cheese Filling	13
Sassafras Tea	6
Sausage Stuffed Jalapenos	12
Soiree Punch	6
Spinach Dip	14
Sweet and Sour Party Meatballs	12
Sweet Tea	6
Tequila Lime Punch	9
Texas Sun Tea	6
Tuna Sandwiches	16

Soups, Salads, & Vegetables

9E Ranch Cowboy Soup	20
Apple Salad	29
Aunt Mae's Fried Potatoes	40
Aunt Opal's Potato Salad	43
Baked Cushaw Squash	44
Bean Salad	28
Brenda's Cream of Broccoli Soup	21
Brenda's Oven-Baked Brandied Cranberries	45
Brenda's Spicy Vegetable Soup	26
Brenda's Wilted Lettuce Salad	31
Calabacitas (Skillet Squash)	37
Cherry Delight	30
Chicken Corn Chowder	23
Chuck Wagon Beans	42
Collier Road Pineapple Bake	30
Corn Pudding	37
Corn Pudding	39
Corn Vegetable Medley	45
Country Seasoned Greens	39
Cowboy Stew	21
Creamy Potato Soup	19
Deviled Eggs	34
Dog Bite Chili	22
Dorothy's Potatoes	35
Dove's Nest Tomato Basil Soup	24
Dove's Nest White Chili	25
Egg Salad	27
Favorite Green Beans	38
Fried Cabbage	37
Fried Cucumbers	40
Frito Corn Salad	28
Fruit Delight	33
Granny's Potato Soup	20
Greens	37
Hash Brown Casserole	35
Helen Tucker's Broccoli Salad	32
Hickory Chickens or Morel Mushrooms	40
Isabelle's Potato Cakes	43
Kentucky Fried Corn	36
L.T. Felty's Chili	23
Leather Breeches Beans (Shuck Beans)	38
Mary Roberts' Soup Beans	41
Mary Rust's Bean Chowder	20
Mildred Roberts' Sweet Potato Balls	44
Minestrone Soup	23
Mormon Potato Soup	27
Mother's Fried Turnips	41
Mother's Fruit Salad	30

Mountain Green Beans & Taters	36
My Kentucky Soup Beans	43
Old Fashion Bologna Salad	28
Orange Peas Amandine	44
Oriental Cabbage Salad	33
Pan Fried Apples	42
Peggy's Rice	41
Polk Sallet Greens	41
Potato Soup	19
Senate Bean Soup	24
Sibley Family Reunion Baked Beans	36
Slow-Cooker Macaroni and Cheese	42
Sour Cream Green Beans Casserole	45
Spring Salad	31
Thelma's Sour Cream Cranberry Salad	34
Timer's Cucumber Salad	29
Turnip Greens with Turnips	39
White Chili	22
Wild Raspberry Salad	33

Meat & Main Dishes

Aunt Ola's Chicken Gizzards with Gravy	49
Aunt Quata Sibley's Meat Loaf	56
Belizean Stew Chicken	51
Brenda's Chicken and Dumplings	54
Brenda's Lasagna	57
Cheyenne River Ribs	55
Chicken Casserole	57
Chicken Tetrazzini/Spaghetti	48
Chuck Pot Coca Cola Roast	47
Cooked Mutton	63
Crock Pot Roast	48
Crock-Pot Beef Tips	47
Deb's Dang Tacos	50
Dr. Pepper Pulled Pork Sandwiches	62
Fried Bologna Sandwich	55
Fried Chicken Gizzards	49
Fried Chicken Livers	48
Fried Chicken	62
Fried Frog Legs	58
Fried Mutton	63
Fried Pork Chops	53
Fried Pork Liver and Onions	51
Fried Rabbit	57
Fried Squirrel with Gravy	52
Glazed Country Ham	58
Kentucky Fried Catfish	51
Mom Sibley's Meat Balls	61

Mrs. Duvall's Chicken Casserole	55
Nancy's Meatballs	67
Nancy's Sloppy Joes	53
Neck Bones	52
Pop Sibley's Texas Chicken-Fried Steak	61
Poppy Seed Chicken	60
Roast Raccoon	62
Salmon Patties	47
Shrimp Scampi	59
Squirrel and Dumplings	52
Teriyaki Salmon	59
Tole Roberts' Meat Loaf	56
Venison Steak	58

Breads, Rolls, & Pastries

10 Minute German Chocolate Pie	84
Anzac Biscuits	67
Apple Cake Bread	74
Brenda's Apple Pie	87
Aunt Quata's Angel Biscuits	66
Banana Nut Bread	74
Banana Pudding	86
Beer Bread	66
Boone Tavern Corn Sticks	75
Boone Tavern Spoon Bread	75
Brenda's Sour Cream Cornbread	70
Butterscotch Pie	87
Buttery Cheesy Chive Muffins	68
Cleo's Pineapple Pie	84
Cornbread Dressing	78
Cranberry Nut Bread	73
Dried Apple Fried Pies	82
Easy Buttermilk Biscuits	72
Five Minute Key Lime Pie	84
Golden Lamb Shaker Sugar Pie	83
Grandma Ida Begley's Cornbread	69
Hemmer Roberts' Hoe Cake-Corn Dodger	71
Homestead Cornbread	65
Indiana Cream Pie	79
Isabelle's Cornbread	69
Jefferson Davis Pie	80
Kentucky Bread Pudding with Bourbon Sauce	89
Mandarin Orange and Cranberry Muffin Bread	73
Mexican Cornbread	72
Lemon Pie	85
Mother's Batty Cakes	69
Mother's Chocolate Cream Pie	78
Mother's Corn Fritters	72
Mother's Muffins	71

Orange Date Pecan Bread	68
Pecan Brownies	86
Quick and Easy Yeast Rolls	65
Sour Cherry Pie	88
Sweet Potato Pie	80
Texas Pecan Pie	79
Texas Pie (Smith County, Texas)	81
Transparent Pie	86
Ulysses Creek Blackberry Cobbler	86
Zucchini Bread	76

Cakes, Cookies, & Desserts

Almond Cream Cheese Pound Cake	121
Angie's Bourbon Balls	134
Apple Nut Cake	105
Aunt Quata's Buttermilk Pound Cake	95
Better Than (Sex) Cake	101
Black Walnut Fudge	138
Blackberry Dumplings	104
Brenda's Apple Crisp	95
Brenda's Southern Comfort Cake	111
Brown Sugar Black Walnut Cake	108
Chocolate-Peanut Butter Amaretto	124
Cocoa Pound Cake	110
Coconut Bon Bon's	129
Coconut Cream Layer Cake	102
Coconut Pecan Praline Cookies	128
Country House Fudge	134
Crisp Peanut Butter Cookies	127
Daisy's Blackberry Cake	100
Date Loaf Candy	139
Dried Apple Stack Cake	116
Eva Jennings' Blackberry Cake	93
Fresh Rhubarb Cake	101
Fruit Cake	119
German Apple Cake	118
German Sweet Chocolate Cake	120
Hershey's Fudge	136
Holiday Chocolate Haystacks	133
Homemade Reese's Bars	127
Italian Cream Cake	112
Jamaican Rum Cake	109
Jewish Apple Cake	106
Joe Frogger Cookies	131
Kentucky Cream Candy	140
Kentucky Pecan Bourbon Cake	91
Lemon Poppy Seed Bundt Cake	92
Linda Kekauoha's Hot Milk Cake	107
Lou Gibson's Blackberry Cake	96

Lou Gibson's Old-Time Gingerbread	122
Mamie Eisenhower's Fudge	136
Martha Couch's Old Fashion Pan Gingerbread	123
Me maw's Blackberry Wine Cake	92
Million Dollar Fudge	135
Minnie Reed's Raw Apple Cake	117
Mother's Bull Nelson Rum Cake	103
Mother's Chocolate No-Cook Cookies	129
Mother's Potato Candy	132
Mrs. Vasiloff's Nutty Noodles	133
Oatmeal Cake	97
Oatmeal Crisps	126
Old Fashion Banana Pudding	125
Old Fashion Sargum Molassie Cookies	130
Old Fashion Stack Cake	114
Old-Time Gingerbread	131
One Bowl Chocolate Cake	110
Peanut Blossoms	128
Peanut Butter Fudge	138
Pecan Brownies	96
Peppermint Fudge	137
Red Velvet Cake	94
See's Fudge	135
Snicker Doodles	126
Solera Cream Sherry Cake	97
Sugar Free Orange Cake	113
Sweet & Salty Delights	132
Texas Sheet Cake	99
The Original Kentucky Whiskey Cake	115
Unusual Fudge	137
White Chocolate Christmas Haystacks	133
Woman's Day Chocolate Cake	113
Xmas Cocoa Fudge	132

Canning & Preserving

Apricot Jam	148
Brenda's Crock Pot Apple Butter	144
Candied Jalapenos/Cowboy Candy	151
Canning Tomatoes	145
Cherry Preserves	143
Chow-Chow	144
Elderberry Jelly	147
Fig Jam	148
Fig Strawberry Preserves	149
Grandmother's Salt Pickles	151
Green Tomato Pickles	146
Mustang Grape Jelly	142

Old-Fashioned Whole Fig Preserves	150
Pepper Jelly	147
Pickled Beets	152
Pickled Peaches	145
Pickled Sweet Onions	152
Polk Stalk Pickles	149
Pomegranate Jelly	142
Refrigerator Pickles	153
Sand Plum (Wild Plum) Jelly	143
Strawberry-Rhubarb Jam	146
Tole Roberts' Kraut	153

This & That

Cornmeal Gravy	155
Tomato Gravy	155
Confectioner's Frosting	156
Chocolate Gravy	155
Maudie's Glazed Pecans	156
Sugared Pecans	156
Chiles Gureos Rellenos Y Asados	157
Amish Church Peanut Butter Spread	157
French Toast	157
Mother's Red Eye Gravy	155
Lemon Dressing	157
Framboise (Raspberry) Sauce	158
Mayan Salsa Habanero Sauce	158
Bourbon Cranberries	159
Florence Begley Cochran's Popcorn Balls	159
Tommie Worthy's Caramel Pecans	160

Made in the USA
Lexington, KY
11 September 2019